RENEW INTERNATIONAL

WHY CATHOLIC?
JOURNEY THROUGH THE CATECHISM

Live

RENEW
INTERNATIONAL

The publisher gratefully acknowledges use of the following:

Scripture quotations from the *New Revised Standard Version Bible* (containing the Old and New Testaments with the Apocryphal/Deuterocanonical Books), © 1989 by the Division of Christian Education of the National Council of the Churches of Christ in the U.S.A., used with permission. All rights reserved.

English translation of the *Catechism of the Catholic Church for the United States of America* © 1994, United States Conference of Catholic Bishops–Libreria Editrice Vaticana. English translation of the *Catechism of the Catholic Church:* Modifications from the *Editio Typica* © 1997, United States Conference of Catholic Bishops–Libreria Editrice Vaticana. Used with permission.

The United States Catholic Catechism for Adults © 2006 United States Conference of Catholic Bishops. Used with permission.

For online access to an interactive site allowing users to search the full text of the *Catechism of the Catholic Church,* go to: www.vatican.va/archive/ENG0015/_INDEX.HTM

Quote from Madeleine Delbrêl in Session 5 from *Blessed Among All Women*, Robert Ellsberg, p. 45. The Crossroads Publishing Co., New York. 2005. All rights reserved.

Quote from Father Pedro Arrupe in Session 6 from *One Jesuit's Spiritual Journey: Autobiographical Conversations with Jean-Claude Dietsch, SJ,* cited in *My Life with the Saints*, James Martin SJ, p.108. Loyola Press. Chicago. 2006. All rights reserved.

The English translation of the *Gloria in excelsis* from *The Roman Missal* © 2010, International Commission on English in the Liturgy Corporation. All rights reserved.

Quote from Bishop Anthony B. Taylor in Session 8 from pastoral letter *Welcome the Strangers Among Us*, November 5, 2008, website of the Diocese of Little Rock. Used with permission.

Quote from Sister Mary Ann Walsh in Session 10 from *Tuscon: Time to Wake Up and Tone Down*, USCCB Media Blog, , January 11, 2011, usccbmedia.blogspot.com. Used with permission.

Citation of Mother Joseph in Session 11 from the web site of the Cowgirls Hall of Fame, Fort Worth, Texas, www.cowgirl.net.

All of the quotes from papal and conciliar documents used in this book are from the English translation as presented by the Vatican website, www.vatican.va.

NIHIL OBSTAT
Monsignor James M. Cafone, S.T.D.
Censor Librorum

IMPRIMATUR
Most Reverend John J. Myers, J.C.D., D.D.
Archbishop of Newark

Cover design by James F. Brisson;
Book design and layout by Kathrine Forster Kuo

Copyright © 2002, 2005, 2007, 2011, 2014
by RENEW International

ISBN 978-1-935532-62-0
(2007 edition ISBN 978-1-935532-02-6)

RENEW International
1232 George Street
Plainfield, NJ 07062-1717
Phone: 908-769-5400
Fax: 908-769-5560
www.renewintl.org
www.WhyCatholic.org

Printed and bound in the United States of America.

Contents

Acknowledgments

RENEW International gratefully acknowledges those who have contributed to this work:

Piloters

Small Christian community members who piloted the materials and offered helpful insights.

Music References

All of the songs suggested in this book are available on a CD produced by RENEW International. See more details on page 114; full details at **www.renewintl.org/store**

The publishers of copyright songs suggested in this book are:

GIA Publications, Inc.
7404 South Mason Avenue
Chicago, IL 60638
Phone 800-442-1358 or 708-496-3800
Fax 708-496-3828
Website www.giamusic.com
E-mail custserv@giamusic.com

Oregon Catholic Press Publications
5536 NE Hassalo
Portland, OR 97213
Phone 800-LITURGY (548-8749)
Fax 800-4-OCP-FAX (462-7329)
Website www.ocp.org
E-mail liturgy@ocp.org

Maranatha Music
5409 Maryland Way, Suite 200
Brentwood, TN 37027
Phone 615-371-1320
Fax 615-371-1351
Website www.musicservices.org

World Library Publications
3708 River Road, Suite 400
Franklin Park, IL 60131
Phone 800-566-6150
Website www.wlpmusic.com

Foreword

My calling as a bishop challenges me to ever seek means to assist solid faith formation and growth in holiness. Foundational in meeting this need is the *Catechism of the Catholic Church,* which so magnificently conveys the wisdom of the Holy Spirit in guiding the Church's tradition in following Jesus Christ.

The Introduction to the U.S. bishops' document *Our Hearts Were Burning Within Us* speaks of how disciples of Jesus share in proclaiming the Good News to the entire world.

Every disciple of the Lord Jesus shares in this mission. To do their part, adult Catholics must be mature in faith and well equipped to share the Gospel, promoting it in every family circle, in every church gathering, in every place of work, and in every public forum. They must be women and men of prayer whose faith is alive and vital, grounded in a deep commitment to the person and message of Jesus.

Why Catholic? Journey through the Catechism is well designed to enable this goal to become reality. It faithfully breaks open the contents of the *Catechism* for reflection and assimilation by individuals or participants in small faith-sharing groups. The sharing enables participants to take greater personal ownership of their faith and to move from an inherited faith to deep faith conviction.

This exploration of divinely revealed truth has a formative effect on peoples' lives. The "yes" of consent to faith emulates Mary's fiat, her "yes" to God's will. A prayerful openness to God's will is the path to holiness.

Why Catholic? seeks to be an instrument for faith formation and a call to holiness. Saints in everyday life are the strength of the Church, which is always renewing itself in fidelity to the mission of Christ and in service to the needs of our society. I heartily commend this effort in making the *Catechism of the Catholic Church* more accessible to the faithful.

Most Reverend John J. Myers, J.C.D., D.D.
Archbishop of Newark

Presenting RENEW International

Why Catholic? Journey through the Catechism is a four-year process of evangelization and adult faith formation developed by RENEW International.

The RENEW process, both parish-based and diocesan-wide, was first developed and implemented in the Archdiocese of Newark, New Jersey. Its success there led other dioceses, in the United States, and in other countries, to bring RENEW to their people and parish communities. In the three decades since its vibrant beginnings, RENEW International has touched the lives of 25 million people in over 150 dioceses in the United States and 23 countries throughout the world. RENEW International has grown organically from its original single RENEW process. Materials and training have been offered in over 40 languages—not just translated but adapted to specific cultures. We have added specific pastoral outreach to campuses, and to young adults in their 20s and 30s. We have incorporated prison ministry, and provided resources for the visually impaired.

The very core of all of these processes remains the same: to help people become better hearers and doers of the Word of God. We do this by encouraging and supporting the formation of small communities who gather prayerfully to reflect on and share the Word of God, to make better connections between faith and life, and to live their faith more concretely in family, work, and community life.

As a not-for-profit organization, our pastoral outreach is sustained in part from the sales of our publications and resources, and the stipends we receive for the services provided to parishes and dioceses. However, our priority is always to serve all parishes who desire to renew their faith and build the Church, regardless of their economic situation. We have been able to fulfill this mission not only in the inner city and rural areas in the United States, but also in the developing world, especially Latin America and Africa, thanks to donations and charitable funding.

As you meet in your small group, we invite you to take a few moments to imagine the great invisible network of others, here in the United States and on the other continents. They gather, as you do, in small Christian communities, around the Word of God present in the Scripture, striving to hear and act upon that Word. Keep them in your prayer: a prayer of thanksgiving for the many graces we have experienced; a prayer that the Spirit will guide all of us as we explore *Why Catholic?*

Introduction

Welcome to *Why Catholic? Journey through the Catechism.*

This four-book series was developed by RENEW International to provide a faith-sharing process for small communities, while unfolding the riches of the *Catechism of the Catholic Church* and the *United States Catholic Catechism for Adults*, both of which are published by the United States Conference of Catholic Bishops. By using these materials, we hope participants will be encouraged to study both catechisms in even greater depth, allowing the teachings within to illuminate their faith and promote an active response in love.

You are about to journey forward with *LIVE: Christian Morality.* This book explores how we live each day according to the teaching of Jesus, especially in the Great Commandments and the Beatitudes.

Why Catholic? is designed to highlight select teachings around which faith sharing may take place, rather than as a compendium or total summary of the catechisms. By nourishing and strengthening women and men in all callings, *Why Catholic?* can serve as an essential tool on the journey to mature Christian faith. We hope that the process will also enable participants to discover and embrace their own

personal faith stories and allow them to reflect on, and answer, the questions, "What does it mean to be Catholic? How did I become Catholic? Why do I remain Catholic?"

Why Catholic? is also designed to balance prayer, sharing on Scripture, and reflection on the teachings of our faith, providing a full and fruitful faith-sharing experience for participants. While a prayerful listening to and reflection on Scripture is an integral part of each session, *Why Catholic?* is not meant to be a Scripture study.

Why Catholic? is designed to correspond to the four pillars of the *Catechism of the Catholic Church* and its complement, the *United States Catholic Catechism for Adults.* The three other books in the *Why Catholic?* series are: *BELIEVE: Profession of Faith; CELEBRATE: Sacraments; and PRAY: Christian Prayer.* If you are gathering in a small community, you may wish to meet either in two six-week blocks of time or during twelve consecutive weeks to allow one week per session.

In addition, we recommend participants keep a journal and, following each session, spend some time journaling key beliefs of the Catholic faith, along with their personal insights. The journal may serve as a valuable meditation tool as well as a springboard for sharing faith with others.

Throughout the *Why Catholic?* series, direct reference is made to both the *Catechism of the Catholic Church* and the *United States Catholic Catechism for Adults*. This material is identified as (*CCC*) and (*USCCA*) respectively. An excellent explanation of the relationship between the two catechisms can be found at the website of the United States Catholic Conference of Bishops: www.usccbpublishing.org/client/client_pdfs/Q&A_on_USCCA.pdf

We pray that your experience with *Why Catholic?* will lead to a closer, more vibrant relationship with our loving God and your community of faith.

Faith-Sharing Principles and Guidelines

When we gather as Christians to share our faith and grow together in community, it is important that we adhere to certain principles. The following Theological Principles and Small Community Guidelines will keep your community focused and help you to grow in faith, hope, and love.

Principles

- God leads each person on his or her spiritual journey. This happens in the context of the Christian community.

- Christ, the Word made flesh, is the root of Christian faith. It is because of Christ, and in and through him, that we come together to share our faith.

- Faith sharing refers to the shared reflections on the action of God in one's life experience as related to Scripture and the faith of the Church. Faith sharing is not discussion, problem solving, or Scripture study. The purpose is an encounter between a person in the concrete circumstances of his or her life and a loving God, leading to a conversion of heart.

- The entire faith-sharing process is an expression of prayerful reflection.

Guidelines

- Constant attention to respect, honesty, and openness for each person will assist the community's growth.

- Each person shares on the level where he or she feels comfortable.

- Silence is a vital part of the total process. Participants are given time to reflect before any sharing begins, and a period of comfortable silence might occur between individual sharings.

- Persons are encouraged to wait to share a second time until others who wish to do so have contributed.

- The entire community is responsible for participating and faith sharing.

- Confidentiality is essential, allowing each person to share honestly.
- Action flowing out of the small community meetings is essential for the growth of individuals and the community.

A Note to Small Community Leaders

Small Community Leaders are ...

- People who encourage participation and the sharing of our Christian faith.
- People who encourage the spiritual growth of the community and of its individual members through communal prayer, a prayerful atmosphere at meetings, and daily prayer and reflection on the Scriptures.
- People who move the community to action to be carried out between meetings. They are not satisfied with a self-centered comfort level in the community but are always urging that the faith of the community be brought to impact on their daily lives and the world around them.
- Community builders who create a climate of hospitality and trust among all participants.

Small Community Leaders are not ...

- Theologians: The nature of the meeting is faith sharing. Should a theological or scriptural question arise, the leader should turn to the pastor or staff to seek guidance.
- Counselors: The small communities are not intended for problem solving. This is an inappropriate setting to deal with emotionally laden issues of a personal nature. The leader is clearly not to enter the realm of treating people with emotional, in-depth feelings such as depression, anxiety, or intense anger. When someone moves in this direction, beyond faith sharing, the leader should bring the community back to faith sharing. With the help of the pastor or staff, the person should be advised to seek the assistance of professional counseling.
- Teachers: The leaders are not teachers. Their role is to guide the process of the faith sharing as outlined in the materials.

N.B. *SOWING SEEDS: Essentials for Small Community Leaders* provides a comprehensive collection of pastoral insights and practical suggestions to assist small community leaders in their crucial role of facilitating a *Why Catholic?* small community. Available from RENEW International's secure online webstore: www.renewintl.org/store

How to Use This Book

Whenever two or more of us gather in the name of Jesus, we are promised that Christ is in our midst (see Matthew 18:20). This book helps communities to reflect on the Scriptures, the *Catechism of the Catholic Church* and the *United States Catholic Catechism for Adults*. It is most helpful if some members of the group or the group as a whole have the Scriptures and one, or both, of the catechisms at their meeting.

Those who have met in small communities will be familiar with the process. In this book based on the *Catechism*, however, there is particular emphasis on the great mysteries of our faith. These reflections make demands upon our reflective nature and help in the formation of our Catholic values. **Therefore, it is important that participants carefully prepare for the session before coming to the meeting.** They are encouraged to read and reflect on the session itself, the Scripture passage(s) cited, and the sections or pages of the *CCC* and the *USCCA* referenced.

If the community has not met before or if participants do not know each other, take time for introductions and to get acquainted. People share most easily when they feel comfortable and accepted in a community.

Prayer must always be at the heart of our Christian gatherings. Following any necessary Introductions, sessions begin with a time of prayer—Lifting Our Hearts. There are suggested songs, but other appropriate songs may be used. All of the suggested songs are available on the CD *Live: Songs for Faith Sharing*, produced by RENEW International. Most of these songs can be found in the standard parish worship collections. If songs are copyrighted, remember you need to request permission before making copies of either the words or the music. The contact information for permissions can be found on page iv.

Each week, an action response— Living the Good News—is recommended. After the first week, the leader encourages participants to share how they put their faith in action by following through on their Living the Good News commitment from the previous session.

Following Lifting Our Hearts, and Living the Good News, there is an initial reflection on the *Catechism* entitled Reflection 1. The next section, Pondering the Word, offers a Scripture reference that one participant proclaims aloud from the Bible. Together, the *Catechism* and Scripture selections will give the community members the opportunity to reflect on what Jesus has said and to share their faith on the particular topic. Sharing could take about 15 minutes.

Next, the small community continues Reflection 2 and then considers the Sharing Our Faith questions. Faith-sharing groups vary greatly in their background and composition. In some sessions, the group may wish to start with the question: What insights into my faith did I gain from this session? Explain. Allow approximately 25 minutes for Sharing Our Faith, making sure the last question is always considered.

In coming to closure, each session offers some ideas for an individual or group action—Living the Good News. Here, participants reflect on how God is inviting them to act during the coming week—how to bring their faith into their daily lives. The ideas presented are merely suggestions. It is important that group members choose an action that is both measurable and realistic.

Each session then concludes with Lifting Our Hearts.

How we can pray right from our hearts

As we gather with others, we are sometimes invited to offer spontaneous prayers. You will be invited to do so several times during these sessions. There is a widely used practice that can make it easier to compose a prayer on the spot; it begins with remembering the words *you, who, do,* and *through.* These words represent familiar elements in prayer.

You: We begin our prayers by addressing and praising God with one of several traditional titles such as "Almighty God," "Ever-loving God," "Heavenly Father," or "Dear Lord."

Who: We acknowledge what God has done for the world and for us. This could include such statements as "who created us to love and serve you," "who give us grace in your sacraments," "who gave your only Son to save us from sin and death," "who made the world with all of its wonders," or "who gathered us here to serve your people."

Do: We ask God to do something for us, for others, or for the world at large: "help us to teach our students with wisdom and gentleness," "help those who do not enjoy economic or political freedom," "help us to respond to the needs of the poor," or "quiet our minds and hearts as we experience this retreat."

Through: We pray through Jesus and with the Holy Spirit.

And so, for example, a person who is invited to offer an opening prayer at a meeting of Catholic school parents might say, "Almighty God, who gave us your only Son as our first and best teacher, help us in what we say and what we do to faithfully pass on his teaching to our children. We ask this through Jesus Christ, our Lord, who lives and reigns with you and the Holy Spirit now and forever. Amen."

Liturgical colors can add to prayerful atmosphere

When we gather for faith sharing, it is important to be in a prayerful and reflective environment. At the beginning of each session of this process, there are suggestions for displaying on a small table the Bible, a candle, and other symbolic items that might contribute to a suitable atmosphere.

In each session, one suggestion is to decorate the table with the color of the liturgical season. The liturgical colors are white, violet, green, red, black, and rose. The Roman Missal prescribes the color to be used in the three liturgical seasons and on specific days, such as Passion Sunday and Pentecost, when the liturgical color is red. In general, however, the colors are white for the Easter and Christmas seasons and on holy days including the Assumption (August 15), the Ascension (forty days after Easter), All Saints (November 1), and the Immaculate Conception (December 8); violet during Lent and Advent; and green during Ordinary Time.

Sharing beyond the Small Community

As a community, you will be using this book as the focus for your sharing. You should consider how the fruits of your sharing can be taken beyond the confines of this group. For example, if you are parents, you could be asking what part of your faith exploration can be shared with your children. RENEW International has designed a resource, entitled RENEWING FAMILY FAITH, to help you achieve exactly this.

RENEWING FAMILY FAITH offers a two-page full-color bulletin for every session contained in the Why Catholic? faith-sharing books. You will find a full description of this invaluable resource on pages 114.

Suggested Format of the Sharing Sessions (1½ hours)

Introductions (when the group is new or when someone joins the group)

Lifting Our Hearts	10 minutes
Sharing the Good News	5 minutes
Reflection 1	10 minutes
Scripture: Pondering the Word and Sharing Question	15 minutes
Reflection 2	10 minutes
Sharing Our Faith	25 minutes
Living the Good News	10 minutes
Lifting Our Hearts	5 minutes

Freedom and Responsibility

Suggested Environment

You may have a Bible and a candle on a small table, with the Bible opened to the Scripture text for this session. Consider decorating the table with the color of the liturgical season. You may also display a large chain in two pieces to represent the moral freedom we exercise when we choose the good.

It is helpful to have available the Catechism of the Catholic Church (CCC) *and the* United States Catholic Catechism for Adults (USCCA).

Lifting Our Hearts

Song Suggestion

"We Are Called," David Haas

Prayer

Pray together

God our Father,
you have called us to act with justice.

You have called us to love tenderly.

You have called us to walk humbly
with you.
As we gather in Christian community,
teach us the power of your ways.

Help us to act justly
in all our interactions and relationships with people.

Teach us how to be in right relationship with ourselves,
with one another,
and with all creation.

We ask for your help,
through Jesus Christ our Lord,
and in the power of the Holy Spirit. Amen.

Reflection 1

We are free to choose

For some of his neighbors, Elvys Guzmán was easy to figure out. The
signs were there. He was Latino–one of the immigrants who were
altering the character of the city and the parish many were used to.
He was dark and burly; he had tattooed arms and pierced ears. And
most of his neighbors didn't know the worst of it. "I was working as
a deejay in a restaurant discotheque," the young Dominican recalled,
gingerly picking his way through his evolving English vocabulary.
"I was using marijuana, but I think somebody gave me something in
a drink, and something was happen to my body. I feel pain. I can't
breathe. Very nervous. And after that I went to the church. I went to
Father Paul, and I said, 'I don't want to live more with this, this kind
of sick. I want to kill my life.' " Father Paul O'Brien, the pastor of
St. Patrick's Church in Lawrence, Mass., dissuaded Elvys, and then
the priest personally counseled Elvys every day. "And after that,"
Elvys said, "I find the love of Jesus Christ." He became active in the
parish–even playing the part of Simon of Cyrene in the elaborate
annual passion play. He took two jobs and enrolled in college, looking
forward to a career in law enforcement. "Some look at me as a
delinquent," Elvys said. "Even Padre Paul teases, 'You have the face
of a gangster!' It's all in fun, but I do acknowledge my past. . . . but all
that really matters is who I am now. My past has died."

(Source: RENEW International's Faith-Sharing Edition DVD of *Scenes from a Parish*, a
documentary film by James Rutenbeck. 2008)

Sharing Question

• Recall and share an instance in which you became aware that
you could choose to change for the better some significant aspect
of your life.

Elvys Guzmán shares a gift that God gave to all of us–one of the
gifts that distinguish us as human beings–the freedom to control
our own actions. Jesus set the example for the use of this gift as, in his
human nature, he freely accepted the will of God even to the point
of dying on the cross. It was, in fact, his sacrifice and his resurrection

and ascension into heaven that won for us the grace we need to live as he lived. Elvys Guzmán experienced this. He went to Father O'Brien in desperation, but with the pastor's guidance, Elvys was touched by grace and saw first of all that he could choose life over death. As he grew in his understanding, he used his personal freedom to choose the good in important aspects of his life.

Unlike creatures that act on instinct, we are able to use our reason to decide what to do or say in any situation, and use our free will to carry out our decision. It is in this sense that we are not like lions and tigers and bears, but instead are like God. God gave us this freedom so that we might, of our own accord, choose to accept his will and ultimately be united with him (*CCC*, 1730). As Elvys' experience illustrates, the more we choose good, the more free we become; we reject the tendency to do wrong that human nature is burdened with because of original sin (*CCC*, 1731-1733).

Of course, having free will means that we are *responsible* for what we do. That is true whenever we act voluntarily. Responsibility for an action can be reduced or even eliminated when we are influenced by such things as ignorance, accident, force, fear, or a psychological impairment, but whenever we *freely* choose our actions we are responsible for them (*CCC*, 1735-1736).

When we exercise this freedom we have to evaluate what we might think or say or do and determine whether it is good or bad. This judgment depends on the moral quality of the act itself; what we intend, what our goal is, in choosing this action; and what circumstances surround the action (*USCCA*, p. 311).

Some acts are always seriously wrong. "Direct killing of the innocent, torture, and rape are examples of acts that are always wrong. Such acts are referred to as intrinsically evil acts, meaning that they are wrong in themselves, apart from the reason they are done or the circumstances surrounding them" (*USCCA*, p. 311). Because the end never justifies the means, therefore, lying cannot be justified as a means of helping another person achieve something good. At the same time, a seemingly good act–such as contributing to charity–can lose its goodness if the donor's only goal is to gain social prominence or political influence. The *Catechism* also points out that the moral quality of an act can be affected by circumstances. In a case of theft, for instance, the seriousness of the wrong can be affected by the amount stolen. And while circumstances–like intentions–cannot change an intrinsically bad act into a good one, they can diminish

3

Spotlight on the *Catechism*

"Freedom is exercised in relationships between human beings. Every human person, created in the image of God, has the natural right to be recognized as a free and responsible being. All owe to each other this duty of respect. The *right to the exercise of freedom*, especially in moral and religious matters, is an inalienable requirement of the dignity of the human person. This right must be protected by civil authority within the limits of the common good and public order" (Cf. DH 2 § 7).

Catechism of the Catholic Church, 1738

or increase the responsibility of the person performing the act (*CCC*, 1754). For example, in Victor Hugo's novel "Les Miserables," the basis for the popular musical play, the central character, Jean Valjean, steals a loaf of bread because his family is in danger of starving. As Hugo implies, the circumstances might have reduced the level of Valjean's guilt. In any event, none of the factors that determine whether or not an act is good can be considered in isolation. "A *morally good* act requires the goodness of the object, of the end, and of the circumstances together" (*CCC*, 1755).

Our human emotions are natural and important aspects of our personalities that often play a part in our choices between good and evil (*CCC*, 1763). These emotions include love, joy, hatred, fear, and sadness. "In themselves, the passions are neither good nor evil," but we govern them in a morally beneficial way through the use of reason (*CCC*, 1767). In other words, our feelings and emotions are good when they urge us toward what is good, and we respond by choosing what is good.

Sharing Question

• Share how you felt after you made a difficult moral decision.

Pondering the Word

The Ten Commandments

Exodus 20:1-17

Sharing Questions

• Take a moment to reflect on what word, phrase, or image from the Scripture passage touches your heart or speaks to your life. Reflect on this in silence, or share it aloud.

• How do the Ten Commandments reflect the Great Commandment of Jesus–love of God and love of neighbor?

Reflection 2

Written in our hearts

The Book of Genesis, the first book of the Bible, tells us that our human nature–with its understanding and free will–is created by God, not by us. In the same way, the moral truths we live by come from God, not from us. As human beings, we have broad freedom to fashion our personal styles and determine how we appear to others. Still, within this freedom, God has given us standards for living as Christians, writing these in our hearts in what is called the natural law. God has also given us the commandments and, through his Son, the Gospel. God has taught us gradually as our minds and hearts have become more sensitive to the work of the Holy Spirit in the Church. There was a time, for example, when much of the Christian community was less aware of the evil of human slavery. As we became more conscious of the sanctity of human freedom and human life, we changed our attitude. In the same way, there is an evolving awareness of the moral dimensions of the impact of human behavior on the physical world. "We need to care for the environment," Pope Benedict XVI has written, "it has been entrusted to men and women to be protected and cultivated with responsible freedom, with the good of all as a constant guiding criterion" (*The Human Family, a Community of Peace*, Letter on the World Day of Peace, 2008). Our goal, therefore, is to live by God's ways, not by our own.

If there were no *objective* sources like the Ten Commandments and the Gospel, morality might become *relative*, and the standard for making any moral decision might become whatever felt right to the person involved. If such expansive personal freedom became the only criterion for making moral choices, it would raise the potential for anyone with power over others to impose his own morality on them. Without an objective standard, they would have no basis for appeal.

But we *do* have a source of moral truth, and Jesus commissioned the Church to speak about it with his authority (*CCC*, 2032). Jesus appointed the apostles and the popes and other bishops who have succeeded them to give Christians direction about moral issues (*CCC*, 2034). In its role as teacher, known as the *magisterium*, the Church alone interprets the word of God, whether in the written form of the Scriptures or in the form of Tradition–the teaching handed down by the apostles and their successors under the guidance of the Holy Spirit (*CCC*, 85-87). However, the whole Christian community shares the

Spotlight on the *Catechism*

"Some believe that due to outside forces, inner compulsions, social pressures, childhood experiences, or genetic makeup, our behavior is already determined and we are not truly free. Though we do recognize that' … responsibility for an action can be diminished or nullified by ignorance, duress, fear, and other psychological or social factors' (CCC, 1746), normally we are still free and responsible for our actions. Our freedom may be limited but it is real nonetheless.

The best way to grow in freedom is to perform good acts. Good deeds help to make us free and develop good habits. The road to loss of freedom is through evil acts. Sin makes us slaves of evil and reduces our capacity to be free. Freedom comes from being moral. Slavery to sin arises from being immoral."

*United States Catholic Catechism
for Adults*, p. 311

mission of spreading the Gospel by faith and example (*CCC*, 2044-2045).

The law of God that is written in our hearts calls us to make the well-being of others more important than our own. Jesus emphasized the importance of this in terms of feeding the hungry, greeting the stranger, clothing the naked, and caring for the sick: "Just as you did it to one of the least of these, who are members of my family, you did it to me" (*Mt* 25:40). So the moral law calls us to love others and equates that with loving God through Jesus. Another way to look at it is that if we fail to love each other, we fail to love God. Jesus, through the grace he offers us, helps us to avoid using others merely as a means of fulfilling our own needs. By opening ourselves to his grace and embracing his teaching, we can follow his example of unconditional caring, sincere giving, and selfless loving.

Our love grows stronger or weaker as we live our lives. In terms of our feelings, we may have periods of closeness and periods of alienation. Sometimes we may feel good about ourselves, and other times we may feel hopeless. Our faith enables us to interpret our experience with the wisdom that comes from God. We learn to "prize the things that are of value" and grow in our understanding of what is important. To live a life that has meaning and purpose, to have intimate relationships that are vital to our happiness, to live a life that is truly human, each of us, by our faith, hope, and love, must have some contact with the invisible reality St. John describes when he says, "God is love" (*1 Jn* 4:8).

Sharing Questions

• We receive moral guidance from the Ten Commandments. What additional guidance do you find in the gospels?

- When did one of the commandments help you to make a difficult decision?
- Describe how gospel values are lived out in your family.

Living the Good News

Jesus emphasized the connection between faith and action, between what we believe and what we do. In that spirit, decide on an individual or group action that flows from what you have shared in this session. If you decide to act on your own, share your decision with the group. If you decide on a group action, determine among you whether individual members will take responsibility for various aspects of the action.

You are likely to benefit most from taking an action that arises from your own response to the session. However, you can consider one of the following suggestions or use these ideas to help develop one of your own:

- Forgive a family member, a friend, or a difficult person who has hurt your feelings. Contact him or her and express your forgiveness.

- Elvys Guzmán tells his story in the documentary film *Scenes from a Parish*, which follows the experiences of parishioners of St. Patrick's Church in the former mill town of Lawrence, Mass. The film examines the challenge of the commandment to love your neighbor when the ethnicity and the social and economic standing of your neighbors are changing–and your city and parish are changing as a result. Introduce your parish to RENEW International's Faith-Sharing Edition DVD of *Scenes from a Parish*, accompanied by a guide to building faith-sharing sessions using the film. Details on page 115.

- Be kind and show interest in a person you feel inclined to treat with coldness or indifference.

- Pray this week with St. John's words, "God is love." Be aware of and pray for any person or situation God brings to your attention.

- Organize a letter-writing campaign in your parish around a particular moral issue–for example, abortion, euthanasia, hunger, or racism. Include your mayor, governor, senator, and representative among to those whom you write.

In light of this session, this week I commit to:

_____

_____

Lifting Our Hearts

Leader　　　Let us pray that the Spirit of God will inspire and encourage us to know and to accomplish the work of the Lord Jesus in our daily lives.

All respond after each petition: **Lord, hear our prayer.**

For the grace to respect others' freedom, we pray. ***R.***

For the grace to become less self-centered and more concerned with the needs of others, we pray. ***R.***

For the grace to love wisely and well the persons you have put into our lives, we pray. ***R.***

Add your own intentions.

To conclude, pray the Lord's Prayer.

Looking Ahead

• Prepare for your next session by prayerfully reading and studying:

  ▪ Session 2: The Beatitudes

  ▪ Matthew 5:3-12

  ▪ *The Collegeville Bible Commentary: New Testament* by Robert J. Karris, for insight into the passage from the Gospel of Matthew.

  ▪ *United States Catholic Catechism for Adults*, Chapter 23 "Life in Christ – Part I," pp. 307-309 on "Jesus the Teacher"

• You may like to consult the relevant paragraphs from the *Catechism of the Catholic Church*:

  ▪ paragraphs 1716-1717 on "The Beatitudes,"

  ▪ paragraphs 1718-1719 on "The Desire for Happiness," and

  ▪ paragraphs 1720-1724 on "Christian Beatitude."

• Remember to use RENEWING FAMILY FAITH and its helpful suggestions on how to extend the fruits of your sharing beyond your group, especially to your families (see page 114).

The Beatitudes

Suggested Environment

You may have a Bible and a candle on a small table, with the Bible opened to the Scripture text for this session. Consider decorating the table with the color of the liturgical season. You also may gather pictures from newspapers and magazines that depict people living the Beatitudes–working for justice, mourning, showing mercy, and so forth. At the beginning of the session, discuss the pictures and make the connection to the Beatitudes.

It is helpful to have available the Catechism of the Catholic Church (CCC) *and the* United States Catholic Catechism for Adults (USCCA).

Lifting Our Hearts

Song Suggestion

"Lead Me, Lord," John D. Becker

Prayer

Pray together

Eternal God,
As we come together in this Christian community,
we thank you for the gift of your Son.

By his example he showed us
how we might live at peace with you
and with the whole world.

In his teaching, he promised blessedness
to all who conformed to your will
by being a blessing to others and to the earth.

Through his death, resurrection, and ascension,
he gained for us the grace that we need
to freely follow him and, through him,
be united with you forever. Amen.

Sharing Our Good News

Before continuing, talk briefly about the results of your plan for Living the Good News *after the last session.*

Reflection 1

A promise of "blessedness"

In 1979, a group of American journalists was visiting Israel on a secular tour. Because a handful of the journalists were Christians, the guide added a few Christian sites to the itinerary. One of those sites was the eight-sided Church of the Beatitudes, overlooking the Sea of Galilee near Tabgha, in the area where tradition says Jesus preached the Sermon on the Mount. As the journalists gathered on the grass outside the church, the guide briefly explained the significance of the place, and then he pulled from his bag a tattered edition of the New Testament. He opened it to a page he had marked, handed it to one of the Christian journalists, and asked him to read the passage aloud. When the man was done reading, many of his colleagues said they had never heard the passage before, and they remarked not only on its beauty but on the power of its message. The passage was St. Matthew's account of the Beatitudes, the centerpiece of the Sermon on the Mount.

Sharing Question

- What qualities of the Beatitudes do you think would make them universally appealing, as they were to members of the tour group who had never heard them before?

We Catholic Christians believe in God, and we want to live according to his will. God has revealed his will to us over time, and he has revealed it most clearly in his Son, Jesus, who said, "I am the way, and the truth, and the life" (*Jn* 14:6) By that, Jesus meant that he is the one connection between God and us. And so, in his ministry on earth, Jesus revealed God's will to us in terms that have to do with everyday life. He told us that just as we are the beloved daughters and sons of God, we must treat each other–treat *all* people– as members of that family. "The most basic principle of the Christian moral life is the awareness that every person bears the dignity of being made in the image of God" (*USCCA*, p. 310). Jesus made that clear–brushing aside traditional distinction of background, religion, gender, and occupation. As we hear in the Beatitudes, he called on us to imitate him in his humility, his compassion, and his acceptance of the will of God.

It was in Jesus, who set this example for us, that God restored human nature to the dignity that had been "disfigured . . . by the first sin" (*CCC*, 1701). Man and woman had been created in the "image" and "likeness" of God (*Gn* 1:26). This means that we, unlike any other creature on earth, were made with a soul that would not die, the ability to understand the world around us (*CCC*, 1704), and a free will with which we are capable of choosing what is good over what is evil (*CCC*, 1704). Through reason, we recognize the voice of God calling us to make that choice again and again in the circumstances that arise in daily life. "Everyone is obliged to follow this law, which makes itself heard in conscience and is fulfilled in the love of God and of neighbor" (*CCC*, 1706). Conforming ourselves to God's will is often difficult; that is a consequence of original sin. We humans are divided within ourselves; as a result, human life, "both individual and social, shows itself to be a struggle, and a dramatic one, between good and evil, between light and darkness" (*Gaudium et spes* 13§1) (*CCC*, 1707). Jesus, by his death and resurrection, overcame the results of original sin, and it is only through him that we can succeed in the struggle to do good and resist evil. Through our faith in him we receive grace, new life, in the Holy Spirit. Through grace we receive eternal life in heaven (*CCC*, 1708-1709).

Spotlight on the *Catechism*

"The word *Beatitude* refers to a state of deep happiness or joy. These Beatitudes are taught by Jesus as the foundations for a life of authentic Christian discipleship and the attainment of ultimate happiness. They give spirit to the Law of the Ten Commandments and bring perfection to moral life. That spirit is ultimately the spirit of love."

United States Catholic Catechism for Adults, pp. 308-309

"Beatitude" means "blessedness," and the promises of blessedness Jesus made in his Sermon on the Mount are at the heart of his teaching (*CCC*, 1716). The Beatitudes reveal the Lord's profound love, and they describe the behavior and attitudes that constitute a Christian life. In the Beatitudes, Jesus cites the Ten Commandments, but "goes beyond them and calls for a radical detachment from material goods and [for] their distribution to the poor" (*USCCA*, p. 308). The *Catechism* calls the Beatitudes "paradoxical promises," because their promise of blessedness to the peaceful and the humble may contradict the expectations of the secular world (*CCC*, 1717) in which the aggressive and the strong often seem to prevail.

Sharing Question

• How has Jesus helped you in the struggle to do good and resist evil?

Pondering the Word

"Your reward is great in heaven"

Matthew 5:3-12

Sharing Questions

• Take a moment to reflect on what word, phrase, or image from the Scripture passage touches your heart or speaks to your life. Reflect on this in silence, or share it aloud.

• When did you, or someone you know, live out one of the Beatitudes in a concrete way?

Reflection 2

Free to choose good over evil

In the Beatitudes, Jesus expresses the goal of our existence. He calls us to fulfill our Baptismal vocation with lives of charity and justice, lives devoted to joyfully and courageously bearing witness to our faith and serving God by serving each other. In Confirmation, the Holy Spirit fortifies us for this vocation with the gifts of wisdom, understanding, right judgment, courage, knowledge, reverence, and awe in the presence of God–the gifts that formed the character of Jesus himself. Jesus calls us to imitate his life, and he addresses his call to each of us personally and to the Church as a whole (*CCC*, 1719). He promises that if we live individually and together in keeping with this vocation, we will have eternal life in the company of the Holy Trinity (*CCC*, 1720-1721).

To achieve this–to "see God," as the sixth Beatitude promises–we have to make moral choices. We have to resist the "bad instincts" that plague our human nature. We have to seek our happiness in the love of God, and not in "riches or well-being, in human fame or power, or in any human achievement–however beneficial it may be–such as science, technology, and art, or indeed in any creature" (*CCC*, 1723).

Writing on that same theme, Cardinal John Henry Newman, a 19th century theologian, cautioned specifically against a temptation that perhaps has grown even more pervasive with the expansion of electronic media. In an era before reality TV and YouTube celebrities, Cardinal Newman wrote, "Notoriety, or the making of a noise in the world–it may be called 'newspaper fame'–has come to be considered a great good in itself, and a ground of veneration" (John Henry Cardinal Newman, "Saintliness the Standard of Christian Principle," in *Discourses to Mixed Congregations* [London: Longmans, Green and Co., 1906] V, 89-90) (*CCC*, 1723).

At one time or another, we all may experience the attraction of these potential evils. We may be tempted to adopt the wrong attitude or to say and do the wrong things. We may be tempted to be indifferent to, or even dismiss, the needs of others and to focus only on ourselves. We may be tempted to manipulate and control people, to use them for our own economic, sexual, or social advantage. When we see ourselves in this light, we may be frustrated by our own weakness.

This is why our Christian faith is so important. We trust that we can do the good and fulfill our baptismal vocation, only through the Paschal Mystery–the death and resurrection and glorification of Jesus Christ. We affirm our faith in this mystery and in the grace it brings us by living in the spirit of the Beatitudes, putting our lives at the service of others and *gratefully* accepting God's will for us.

Sharing Questions

• Where do you turn for support in living out the Paschal Mystery in your own life?

• Which one of the Beatitudes is most challenging for you, for your family, for our times? Why?

• How does your life reflect your faith that Jesus is calling you personally?

Spotlight on the *Catechism*

"But we should always remember that Christ's dying and rising offers us new life in the Spirit, whose saving grace delivers us from sin and heals sin's damage within us. Thus we speak of the value, dignity, and goal of human life, even with its imperfections and struggles. Human life, as a profound unity of physical and spiritual dimensions, is sacred. It is distinct from all other forms of life, since it alone is imprinted with the very image of its Creator."

United States Catholic Catechism for Adults, page 310

Living the Good News

Jesus emphasized the connection between faith and action, between what we believe and what we do. In that spirit, decide on an individual or group action that flows from what you have shared in this session. If you decide to act on your own, share your decision with the group. If you decide on a group action, determine among you whether individual members will take responsibility for various aspects of the action.

You are likely to benefit most from taking an action that arises from your own response to the session. However, you can consider one of the following suggestions or use these ideas to help develop one of your own:

- Be a blessing to someone this week by going out of your way to be thoughtful and kind.
- Inquire at the municipal building in your town about volunteer opportunities in recreation or senior-citizens programs. If your town doesn't have a volunteer clearinghouse, consider volunteering to start one.
- Read the Gospel of Mark, the earliest and shortest gospel. Consider how you can be more like Jesus as he is presented in the gospel.
- Choose a specific Beatitude that you will work on in the coming month. Record in a journal how you do.
- Speak out more forthrightly about a cultural value that is at odds with the gospel.

In light of this session, this week I commit to:

_____

_____

Lifting Our Hearts

Prayed by alternating groups or by participants on opposite sides of the room:

Group 1   O Holy Spirit,
           teach us and enable us
           to give witness to a culture
           that has forgotten
           you have called us to be
           a God-centered people.

Group 2	Give us the grace to move from consumerism to simplicity, from individualism to concern for others, from materialism to an appreciation of the spiritual and contemplative.
All	**Transform our desires for wealth and power into those qualities that will bring us to your peace and deepen your life in us. We ask this through Jesus Christ our Lord. Amen.**

Conclude by offering spontaneous prayers, thanking God for the simple blessings in your life.

Looking Ahead

- Prepare for your next session by prayerfully reading and studying:
  - Session 3: Forming Our Conscience
  - Romans 2:12-16
  - *The Collegeville Bible Commentary: Old Testament* by Robert J. Karris, for insight into the passage in Romans.
  - *United States Catholic Catechism for Adults*, Chapter 23 "Life in Christ – Part I," pp. 314-315 on "The Formation of Conscience."

- You may like to consult the relevant paragraphs from the *Catechism of the Catholic Church*:
  - paragraphs 1783-1785 on "The Formation of Conscience"
  - paragraphs 1786-1789 on "To Choose in Accord with Conscience"
  - paragraphs 1790-1794 on "Erroneous Judgment"

- Remember to use RENEWING FAMILY FAITH and its helpful suggestions on how to extend the fruits of your sharing beyond your group, especially to your families (see page 114).

Forming Our Conscience

Suggested Environment

You may have a Bible and a candle on a small table, with the Bible opened to the Scripture text for this session. Consider decorating the table with the color of the liturgical season. You may also display a photo or other representation of the Ten Commandments or a picture that represents the Sacrament of Reconciliation.

It is helpful to have available the Catechism of the Catholic Church (CCC) *and the* United States Catholic Catechism for Adults (USCCA).

Lifting Our Hearts

Song Suggestion

"This Alone," Tim Manion

Prayer

Pray together

Lord Jesus Christ, you loved your apostles and revealed your glory to them.

As we gather together in this place, look upon us with patience and mercy.

Grant us the grace to know what is right and to do what is just.

Help us walk in the way of your commandments and to love you in all things and above all things. Amen.

Sharing Our Good News

Before continuing, talk briefly about the results of your plan for Living the Good News *after the last session.*

Reflection 1

A voice that dwells within

When Elisabeth Arrighi was about to marry Felix Leseur in France in 1889, she was startled to learn that he had abandoned the Catholic Church. Although he promised to respect his wife's faith, which was deeply spiritual, he soon began a campaign of argument and ridicule that nearly caused Elisabeth, after seven years, to give up her religious practice. But further study restored her to a devout Christian life. She continued to pray for her husband to be converted, but she died of cancer in 1914 without seeing her hope fulfilled. After her death, Felix learned in a letter she had left for him that she had offered her suffering for his conversion. Moved by that and by her patient endurance of her illness, Felix eventually returned to the Church. In fact, he became a Dominican priest in 1923, and served for 27 years. The cause for canonization of Elizabeth Leseur was begun in 1934.

Sharing Question

• Describe a time when you listened to the voice within rather than the voices in the world around you.

Deep within ourselves we encounter a law that was written there by God. This law–engraved in our conscience–calls us "to love and to do what is good and to avoid evil" (*GS* 16) (*CCC*, 1776). Conscience prompts us to live always in keeping with God's commandments, and it "judges particular choices, approving those that are good and denouncing those that are evil" (Cf. *Rom* 1:32) (*CCC*, 1777). Conscience affirms the freedom God gave us as human beings; it is, the *Catechism* tells us, "a judgment of reason" (*CCC*, 1778) by which we recognize the good of an act we are about to perform, are in the midst of performing, or have already completed. In everything we think, say, and do, we are obliged to follow what we know to be just and right.

In order to be in touch with our conscience, it is important that we have an interior life. That means managing the many distractions of modern life that can keep us from reflection and self-examination.

It means finding times of quiet in order to hear the voice of God. It means prayer. "Return to your conscience, question it," St. Augustine writes. "Turn inward, brethren, and in everything you do, see God as your witness" (St. Augustine, *In ep Jo.* 8,9: PL 35, 2041) (CCC, 1779).

Spotlight on the *Catechism*

"We need to confront the weakening of conscience in modern society. Too many people fail to distinguish between good and evil when dealing with the value of human life. Moral confusion leads many to support choices and policies that desecrate life. Choices that were once considered criminal and immoral have become socially acceptable. Many consciences that were once formed by the Ten Commandments, Christ's moral teachings, and the Holy Spirit's grace-filled guidance are now swayed by the moral confusion of the spirit of the times. We should deal with the weakening of conscience by helping people to understand the Church's teaching on conscience as the capacity to make judgments in agreement with God's law, to protect human dignity and reject anything that degrades it."

United States Catholic Catechism for Adults, p. 390

Conscience enables us to take responsibility for what we say and do. In the event that we do not choose what is good, however, conscience stays with us, reminding us of the right and wrong involved in our choice, but also encouraging us to seek forgiveness from God and–as Felix Leseur did–to choose the good in the future.

"And by this we will know that we are from the truth and will reassure our hearts before him whenever our hearts condemn us; for God is greater than our hearts, and he knows everything" (*1 Jn* 3:19-20) (CCC, 1781).

The Church teaches us that we have not only an obligation but a "right to act in conscience and in freedom so as personally to make moral decisions" (CCC, 1782). That means that no one should be forced to act against conscience or be prevented from acting according to conscience. So, for example, an employer should not compel an employee to treat a customer dishonestly, and a spouse should not try to keep a partner from choosing and practicing a particular religion.

The *Catechism* teaches that we must always act as our conscience tells us (CCC, 1790). Educating our conscience with the moral teaching of the Church "is indispensible for human beings who are subjected to negative influences and tempted by sin to prefer their own judgment and to reject authoritative teachings" (CCC, 1783). This forming of our conscience is a lifelong process in which we actively seek the truth (CCC, 1785). It is very important to remember in this connection that "our conscience .

. . can make a mistake about what is truly the good or the right thing to do. This can be due to ignorance in which, through no fault of our own, we did not have all we needed to make a correct judgment" (*USCCA*, p. 315). So a person who firmly believes that it is sinful to gamble, but gambles anyway, is not acting according to conscience. It is also true that if we have doubts about what is morally good, we have an obligation to seek counsel in order to enlighten our conscience.

Sharing Question

• Name ways in which your conscience has been formed or developed.

Pondering the Word

God judges the secret thoughts

Romans 2:12-16

Sharing Questions

• Take a moment to reflect on what word, phrase, or image from the Scripture passage touches your heart or speaks to your life. Reflect on this in silence, or share it aloud.

• What does this scripture passage tell you about loved ones who do not believe?

Reflection 2

Living by gospel values

It is our conscience, our awareness of ourselves as moral beings, that makes personal relationships possible. We want to become sincere, honest, sensitive, and generous persons, not phony, deceitful, uncaring, or selfish ones. We seek to develop ethical qualities such as altruism and trustworthiness. We want to be hopeful and loyal. We want to be insightful and honest about our own motivations. It is by following the teaching and the example of Jesus that we can grow in understanding, accept the truth about our own lives, and learn to love others as Christ loves us.

In order to keep the Ten Commandments and follow the Beatitudes and the moral teachings of the Church, we are challenged to form our consciences based on gospel values rather than on secular ones. A well-formed Christian conscience will recognize as immoral the actions of those who lie, steal, or are violent with others; those who do not control their sexual drives; those who deliberately abuse alcohol or drugs; those who direct corporations or governments that engage in unjust practices against individuals or societies; those who act without regard for the physical environment.

Spotlight on the *Catechism*

"A good conscience requires lifelong formation. Each baptized follower of Christ is obliged to form his or her conscience according to objective moral standards. The Word of God is a principal tool in the formation of conscience when it is assimilated by study, prayer, and practice. The prudent advice and good example of others support and enlighten our conscience. The authoritative teaching of the church is an essential element in our conscience formation. Finally, the gifts of the Holy Spirit, combined with regular examination of our conscience, will help us develop a morally sensitive conscience."

United States Catholic Catechism for Adults, p. 314

The values of secular society may encourage us to use our energies in the pursuit of pleasure, possessions, power, popularity, and position; yet, Jesus, in the Beatitudes, calls us to a higher standard, urging us to serve the needs of those who are hungry, thirsty, lonely, and oppressed. He calls us to hunger and thirst for justice, to comfort all God's people, to be unwavering and unapologetic about our faith–even when it conflicts with popular mores–and to find rest from our labors by seeking the Lord in and above all earthly concerns.

Contemporary culture may suggest that we should not make moral judgments at all, but respect the autonomy of those whose values differ from our own. For example, much of society may encourage us to accept the sin of abortion as a "right to choose" to end the life of unborn infants. We may also be pressured by society to accept injustice and quiet our consciences about the immoral practices of governments that tolerate the enslaving, maiming, or killing of their minorities, or corporations that make huge profits from unjust labor practices or careless use of natural resources. But the Church teaches that we have a serious responsibility to love our neighbor (CCC, 1789) and an equally serious responsibility to make moral judgments and choose moral actions that will work for the common good (CCC, 1787).

Sharing Questions

- How has your conscience been your guide in choosing the good?

- Describe a time when your decision to do the right thing involved a personal risk. What helped you to make and carry out your decision?

- What family practices and traditions can help children form a right conscience?

Living the Good News

Jesus emphasized the connection between faith and action, between what we believe and what we do. In that spirit, decide on an individual or group action that flows from what you have shared in this session. If you decide to act on your own, share your decision with the group. If you decide on a group action, determine among you whether individual members will take responsibility for various aspects of the action.

You are likely to benefit most from taking an action that arises from your own response to the session. However, you can consider one of the following suggestions or use these ideas to help develop one of your own:

- Reflect on one aspect of your life–for example, marriage, family, work, school, leisure–in which you would like to further form your conscience.

- Read *Blessed Among All Women* by Robert Ellsberg, a collection of meditations inspired by more than sixty women who lived in the spirit of the Beatitudes (The Crossroad Publishing Co., New York. 2005).

- Donate items to a local food bank or volunteer to assist the food bank in other ways, such as soliciting, collecting, sorting, packing, or delivering food.

In light of this session, this week I commit to:

_____

_____

Lifting Our Hearts

Offer spontaneous prayers to Jesus for guidance either in specific decisions you have to make in the near future or for decisions you will have to make as a spouse, parent, minister, volunteer, or employee.

Pray together

Lord Jesus, through your Church
you teach us that love is our origin,
love is our goal,
and love will be our fulfillment in heaven.

Enlighten our minds and open our hearts
to the many challenges of love in our lives.

Help us to seek you and
find you in one another,
especially in those in need. Amen.

Looking Ahead

- Prepare for your next session by prayerfully reading and studying:
    - Session 4: Living a Virtuous Life
    - 1 Corinthians 12:31-13:13
    - *The Collegeville Bible Commentary: New Testament* by Robert J. Karris, for insight into the passages from the first Letter to the Corinthians.
    - *United States Catholic Catechism for Adults*, Chapter 23 "Life in Christ – Part I," page 318 on "Loves, Rules, and Grace."
- You may like to consult the relevant paragraphs from the *Catechism of the Catholic Church*:
    - paragraphs 1803-1845 on the virtues
- Remember to use RENEWING FAMILY FAITH and its helpful suggestions on how to extend the fruits of your sharing beyond your group, especially to your families (see page 114).

SESSION FOUR

Living a Virtuous Life

Suggested Environment

You may have a Bible and a candle on a small table, with the Bible opened to the Scripture text for this session. You may place colorful stones on the Bible–representing the virtues. Consider decorating the table with the color of the liturgical season.

It is helpful to have available the Catechism of the Catholic Church (CCC) *and the* United States Catholic Catechism for Adults (USCCA).

Lifting Our Hearts

Song Suggestion

"Servant Song," Sister Donna Marie McGargill, OSM

Prayer

Pray together

Lord Jesus Christ,
we have gathered in this community
because we seek to know your will
and carry it out in our daily lives.

We often become intensely aware
of the wide disparity between what we should be doing
and what we actually find ourselves doing
in our relationships with family members
as well as those with whom we work and play.

By the work of your Holy Spirit,
give us the insight to face the true motives
for our attitudes, words, and actions.

Help us to overcome our selfishness and envy
so that we may be a blessing to others
rather than a stumbling block to their spiritual growth. Amen.

Sharing Our Good News

Before continuing, talk briefly about the results of your plan for Living the Good News *after the last session.*

Reflection 1

Choosing what is good

It isn't every girl who has an emperor for a godfather, but Frances Schervier did. Her father owned a manufacturing plant in Aachen, Germany, and when Emperor Francis I of Austria visited the factory in 1818, he accepted an invitation to be sponsor for the child, who had not yet been born. When Frances was baptized the following year, there was an imperial proxy on hand. But although her life had that auspicious start, she was still young when tragedy struck. Her mother died in 1832 and two of her sisters in 1833. At 14 years of age, Frances took over the family's domestic affairs for her father and her younger siblings. Serving others out of necessity was consistent with the tendency Frances already had to serve others out of love. Frances gave so much away to the poor that one of the Scherviers' servants worried that the child would empty the house. She even sold the emperor's gifts and gave the proceeds to the poor. When she was 21, she joined a parish women's group that visited the poor and the sick. She joined the Third Order of St. Francis in 1844 and, after her father died, she and four other young women began to live as a community. By 1851, this small group had evolved into the Sisters of the Poor of St. Francis. Elizabeth sent sisters to Cincinnati to minister to German immigrants, and she joined a group of sisters in helping wounded soldiers and displaced civilians during the American Civil War. She and her sisters also staffed ambulances and nursed the wounded during the Franco-Prussian War. Frances declined a medal offered by Empress Elisabeth of Austria, saying the work was done by her community, not by her as an individual. Her work continues in the United States, Europe, and Africa through her original order and the Franciscan Sisters of the Poor. Frances Schervier was beatified by Pope Paul VI in 1974.

Sharing Question

- Frances Schervier was inclined from an early age to give whatever she could to people who were poor. Who among your acquaintances has inspired you by treating their own wealth or possessions as though they belonged to people in need?

Christian life involves cultivating our inclination to do what is good. With the help of the Holy Spirit, this inclination–or virtue– can become a habit that governs our choices and our actions more and more firmly over time (*CCC*, 1803). There are both human and theological virtues, and living a moral life requires the practice of both (*USCCA*, p. 315). A person can acquire human virtues and, where necessary, overcome bad habits, or vices, through constant and disciplined effort. Virtues are related to the human freedom we have already considered: a virtuous person freely does what is good (*CCC*, 1804).

Among the human virtues there are four that play a pivotal part in our lives and, for that reason, are called the "cardinal virtues." They are prudence, justice, fortitude, and temperance (*CCC*, 1805). Prudence guides our consciences to correctly apply moral principles in our daily living (*CCC*, 1806). Justice disposes our hearts and minds to respect the rights of others and promote harmony and equity in human relationships. Justice also inclines us to give to God the love and worship due to him (*CCC*, 1807). Fortitude strengthens us in difficult times and keeps us on the correct path. It helps us to overcome fear and accept the trials and sufferings that come our way as we strive to do what is right (*CCC*, 1808). Temperance gives us mastery over our feelings and appetites and helps us use created goods with balance and moderation (*CCC*, 1809).

While we may acquire these human virtues through our own effort, we do so only with the help of God. "Christ's gift of salvation offers us the grace necessary to persevere in the pursuit of the virtues. Everyone should always ask for this grace of light and strength, frequent the sacraments, cooperate with the Holy Spirit," (*CCC*, 1811), and follow God's call to love what is good and shun what is evil.

Spotlight on the *Catechism*

"The human virtues are also acquired through seeing them in the good example of others and through education in their value and methods to acquire them. Stories that inspire us to want such virtues help contribute to their growth within us. They are gained by a strong will to achieve such ideals. In addition, God's grace is offered to us to purify and strengthen our human virtues, for our growth in virtue can be hampered by the reality of sin. Especially through prayer and the Sacraments, we open ourselves to the gifts of the Holy Spirit and God's grace as another way in which we grow in virtue."

United States Catholic Catechism for Adults, p. 317

Sharing Question

- What human virtues do you wish to strengthen in yourself? What can you do to pursue that goal?

Pondering the Word

Forgive, as God has forgiven

1 Corinthians 12:31-13:13

Sharing Questions

- Take a moment to reflect on what word, phrase, or image from the Scripture passage touches your heart or speaks to your life. Reflect on this in silence, or share it aloud.

- How has the way you make moral decisions changed as you have matured?

Reflection 2

God is our model of love

The theological virtues, unlike the human virtues, are directly implanted in our souls as gifts from God, beginning with our baptism. We do not acquire them by our own effort. The theological virtues–faith, hope, and charity–make us able and incline us to live in a relationship with the Holy Spirit (*CCC*, 1812).

Faith is the virtue by which we believe in God and believe in what he has said–all that is revealed in the Scriptures and all that we are taught by the Church. By faith, we commit ourselves to God and therefore strive to live according to his will (*CCC*, 1814). Faith doesn't mean only passively accepting religious teaching, however; to unite us with Christ, this virtue must be accompanied by good works–that is, charity and justice–and by our efforts to profess and spread the faith (*CCC*, 1815-1816).

Hope is the virtue by which we desire eternal life in the presence of God, trusting in the promises of Jesus and relying on the help of the Holy Spirit. Hope keeps us from being discouraged, sustains us if we feel abandoned, and opens our hearts as we look forward to the blessings the Lord has promised (*CCC*, 1818).

Charity is the virtue by which we love God above all things and love our neighbors as ourselves out of love of God (*CCC*, 1882). "The Lord asks us to love as he does, even our *enemies*, to make ourselves the neighbor of those farthest away, and to love children and the poor as Christ himself" loved them (Cf. *Mt* 5:44; *Lk* 10:27-37; *Mk* 9:37; *Mt* 25:40-45) (*CCC*, 1825).

The virtue of charity animates and inspires all the other virtues in the service of love. Our human ability to believe, to hope, and to love is elevated to a supernatural level by the powerful presence of God's Holy Spirit (*CCC*, 1827, 1830). The Spirit sustains the virtues in us through the gifts of wisdom, understanding, counsel, fortitude, knowledge, piety, and awe in the presence of the Lord.

The importance of the virtue of charity–of love–was emphasized by St. Paul in the familiar passage from his first letter to the Christian community in Corinth. Without love, he wrote, we gain nothing, we are nothing (*1 Cor* 13:2-3). The first Letter of John says that God is love (*1 Jn* 4:8,16), and the Gospel according to John describes the love that unites the Holy Trinity (*Jn* 3:35,5:20)–the Creator, the Savior, and the Spirit. We are in tune with that divine love because of the presence of the Holy Spirit within us. From that unity of Persons we derive the model for our own moral lives, for the way we treat friends, strangers, and enemies.

Spotlight on the *Catechism*

"Each of the Ten Commandments forbids certain sins, but each also points to virtues that will help us avoid such sins. Virtues such as generosity, poverty of spirit, gentleness, purity of heart, temperance, and fortitude assist us in overcoming and avoiding what are called the seven deadly or Capital Sins–pride, avarice or greed, envy, anger, lust, gluttony, and sloth or laziness–which are those sins that engender other sins and vices."

United States Catholic Catechism for Adults, p. 317

Sharing Questions

- St. Paul writes that "faith, hope, and love abide, these three; and the greatest of these is love." Why do you think St. Paul says the greatest of the virtues is love?

- What has contributed to deepening your understanding about what is good and what is bad?

- Our reflection says that faith doesn't mean passively accepting religious teaching. What does faith mean to you?

Living the Good News

Jesus emphasized the connection between faith and action, between what we believe and what we do. In that spirit, decide on an individual or group action that flows from what you have shared in this session. If you decide to act on your own, share your decision with the group. If you decide on a group action, determine among you whether individual members will take responsibility for various aspects of the action.

You are likely to benefit most from taking an action that arises from your own response to the session. However, you can consider one of the following suggestions or use these ideas to help develop one of your own:

- Re-read the section of the *Catechism* that focuses on the virtues (*CCC*, 1803-1845). Choose one virtue and ask the Holy Spirit to strengthen this virtue in you. Write steps in your journal or share with a friend how you intend to work to include this virtue in your life more frequently.

- Re-read the scripture passage in this session (*1 Cor* 12:31-13:13), praying with each of St. Paul's reflections on love.

- Reflect on the Trinity. Which person of the Trinity do you turn to in times of joy, trouble, confusion, and peace? What draws you to this Person of the Trinity? Write in your journal about your feelings or share them with a friend.

- Reflect on the Trinity in relation to the virtues. Draw the image that comes to mind. Consider further expressing that image in a poem, pottery, or photography.

In light of this session, this week I commit to:

_____

_____

Lifting Our Hearts

Take a few minutes to reflect on the people outside of your family and circle of friends for whom you feel the love preached and practiced by Jesus. Offer spontaneous prayers of intercession on behalf of one or more of those people.

Invite two members of the group to be Voices 1 and 2 in this prayer:

All   **Almighty God, fill us with the love of Jesus Christ.**

Voice 1   For, if we speak in the tongues of mortals and of angels, but do not have love, we are only noisy gongs or clanging cymbals.

Voice 2   And if we have prophetic powers, and understand all mysteries and all knowledge, and if we have all faith, so as to remove mountains, but do not have love, we are nothing.

Voice 1   If we give away all our possessions, and if we hand over our bodies so that we may boast, but do not have love, we gain nothing.

Voice 2   Fill us with love that is patient and kind; love that is not envious or boastful or arrogant or rude; love that does not insist on its own way, that is not irritable or resentful.

All   **Fill us with love that does not rejoice in wrongdoing, but rejoices in the truth; love that bears all things, hopes all things, endures all things; love that never ends. Amen.**

Based on 1 Corinthians 13:1-8

Looking Ahead

- Prepare for your next session by prayerfully reading and studying:

  - Session 5: Jesus: The Compassion of God

  - John 4:4-30 (The encounter between Jesus and the Samaritan woman)

  - *The Collegeville Bible Commentary: New Testament* by Robert J. Karris, for insight into the passage from the Gospel of John.

  - *United States Catholic Catechism for Adults*, Chapter 24 "Life in Christ – Part II: The Principles of the Christian Moral Life," on "Consciousness of solidarity and social justice," pages 324-327."

- You may like to consult the relevant paragraphs from the *Catechism of the Catholic Church*:
  - paragraphs 1846-1876 on "sin"
  - paragraphs 1877-1896 on "the person and society"
  - paragraphs 1897-1927 on "participation in social life"
  - paragraphs 1928-1948 on "social justice"
- Remember to use RENEWING FAMILY FAITH and its helpful suggestions on how to extend the fruits of your sharing beyond your group, especially to your families (see page 114).

Jesus: The Compassion of God

Suggested Environment

You may have a Bible and a candle on a small table, with the Bible opened to the Scripture text for this session. Consider decorating the table with the color of the liturgical season. You may also display a paper heart torn into several large pieces. After the faith sharing, tape the pieces together and pray for the healing of all brokenness.

It is helpful to have available the Catechism of the Catholic Church (CCC) *and the* United States Catholic Catechism for Adults (USCCA).

Lifting Our Hearts

Song Suggestion

"Blest Be the Lord," Daniel L. Schutte

Prayer

Pray together

Dear Jesus,
as we come together to reflect on our faith,
embrace us with your love and mercy.
Open us to your Holy Spirit.
Heal our hearts, wounded by sin.
Heal and comfort those we have sinned against.
Help us to see you in all our sisters and brothers.
Teach us to love as you love. Amen.

Offer spontaneous prayers for those from whom you feel separated because of differences in background or belief.

Sharing Our Good News

Share how you did with your Living the Good News *from the previous session.*

Reflection 1

God lives among his people

What Madeleine Delbrêl lacked in size she made up for in fire power. Born in southern France in 1904, she grew to be only four and a half feet tall. Still, she was a bundle of energy whose exuberance for life lit up her surroundings. Madeleine was an atheist in early life but at the age of 24 she concluded that God was real and that she should serve him. Convinced that men and women could experience the presence of God in the most mundane activities of daily life, she and a group of friends established a small lay community in Ivry-sur-Seine, a working-class city south of Paris and a bastion of French Communism. They engaged the working people of the town, who were estranged from the Church, and built up enough mutual trust, enough solidarity, that the local government asked Madeleine to supervise relief efforts for the refugees who poured into the city at the outbreak of World War II–something she did with her usual vigor. Madeleine Delbrêl didn't think all missionaries had to carry the gospel across international borders. She thought there was need enough among the folks nearby who, no matter how they differed from her, were members of the same human family. "We, the ordinary people of the streets," she said, "believe with all our might that this street, this world, where God has placed us, is our place of holiness."

Sharing Question

• What opportunities are there for you to bear witness to the gospel among people in your community who don't share your background or beliefs?

When a Pharisee asked Jesus which commandment was the greatest, Jesus answered, "'You shall love the Lord your God with all your heart, and with all your soul, and with all your mind.' This is the greatest and first commandment. And a second is like it: 'You shall love your neighbor as yourself' " (*Mt* 22:37-40). And Jesus continued to say that the whole Jewish religious law and the teachings of the prophets flowed from those two commandments: love of God and love of other human beings. Jesus said, in other words, that we should live as part of a loving community. This idea is a reflection of the life of God, since the Holy Trinity itself, revealed to us by Jesus, is a loving community–united in love and pouring out love on creation. Furthermore, our union with Jesus Christ and with each other in the Church–the body of Christ–is an expression of the two great commandments.

We sin when we act against these commandments. So we sin when we do not live, as Jesus did, in obedience to God's will, when we do not love God with our whole selves, and when we do not unconditionally love other human beings–family, friends, strangers, and enemies–as God unconditionally loves us.

We read in the gospels that through the death and resurrection of Jesus, God has reached out to forgive our sins. To receive God's forgiveness, we must honestly probe our consciences and admit our faults. We can do this through the Sacrament of Penance, not as though it were only a ritual or a charm, but as an opportunity to have a change of heart–a conversion–receive God's grace, restore our union with him in the Eucharist, and begin life anew (*CCC*, 1846-1848).

What, then, is sin? It is an offense against God. It is disobedience of God's will. It is love of self carried to the extreme of wishing to become like a god by making one's own decisions about good and evil (*CCC*, 1850). Sin is also "an offense against reason, truth, and right conscience" (*CCC*, 1849), an attachment to material goods or to personal ambitions that are contrary to God's will and disdainful of the interests and wellbeing of the human family.

There are many kinds of sin. The Ten Commandments identify broad categories of sin, including blasphemy, theft, murder and other violence, adultery, and envy. St. Paul, in his letter to the Christian community in Galatia, mentions such offenses as jealousy, anger, selfishness, and drunkenness (*Gal* 5:20-21). There are sins against God, against neighbor, and against one's self. There are sins of the body and sins of the mind–that is, of thought. There are sins that consist of things a person does, and sins that consist of things a person neglects to do. In all cases, however, sin is a free decision to act against the will of God (*CCC*, 1853).

Although all sin wounds a person's relationship with God and with other human beings, the Church regards some sins as more serious than others. Specifically, the Church distinguishes between *mortal* sin and *venial* sin. Mortal sin turns a person away from God in such a way that breaks the relationship. Three conditions must be present in order for a sin to be mortal: grave matter, full knowledge, and complete consent of the person's will. Grave matter means that the action or the speech or the thought involved in the sin must be serious.

Full knowledge means that the person knows clearly that what he or she is doing is sinful. Complete consent of the will means that the person is acting voluntarily and is not being forced or misled by some outside influence or hampered by a mental or emotional disorder (*CCC*, 1855-1860).

"Light" sins should be taken seriously

"From any sin, however small, committed with full knowledge, may God deliver us, especially since we are sinning against so great a Sovereign and realizing that He is watching us! That seems to me to be a sin committed of malice aforethought: it is as though one were to say: 'Lord, although this displeases Thee, I shall do it. I know that Thou seest it and I know that Thou wouldst not have me do it; but, though I understand this, I would rather follow my own whim and desire than Thy will.' If we commit a sin in this way, however slight, it seems to me that our offence is not small but very, very great."

St. Teresa of Ávila, *The Way of Perfection*

In venial sin, at least one of the conditions of mortal sin is absent. So a person might commit venial sin because the act itself is not grave–petty gossip, for example–or a person might sin in a serious matter but without either full knowledge of the law or complete consent of the will. A venial sin does not cut a person off from God as mortal sin does, but it harms the relationship. Moreover, a habit of committing venial sin can make a person more likely to commit mortal sin (*CCC*, 1862-1863). Repeated sin encourages the development of vices–bad habits–that are the opposite of the human virtues. These vices can infect not only individuals but businesses, institutions, governments, and social groups in which those who together act immorally or unjustly share the responsibility for each other's actions (*CCC*, 1865-1869).

"Sorrow for sin and confession of sin are signs of conversion of heart that open us to God's mercy" (*USCCA*, p. 313.) We must remember, too, that this mercy is offered not only to us, and we should leave judgment to God when we think another person may have committed serious sin. "This is because one person cannot know the extent of another individual's knowledge and freedom, which are integral factors determining when an occasion for mortal sin becomes an actual sin . . . "(*USCCA*, p. 313).

Sharing Question

• When have you experienced "new life" that comes from celebrating the sacraments of Penance and Holy Eucharist?

Pondering the Word

"Worship him in spirit and in truth"

John 4:4-30

Sharing Questions

• Take a moment to reflect on what word, phrase, or image from the Scripture passage touches your heart or speaks to your life. Reflect on this in silence, or share it aloud.

• What words would you use to describe the way Jesus and the Samaritan woman spoke to each other? What does this conversation teach us about relationships–with other people and with Jesus?

Reflection 2

No one is an island

Human nature requires us to live in society, interacting with each other and helping each other. Each person has an obligation to take part in the life of the larger community. We fulfill that obligation first by taking care of our personal responsibilities; through support and education of our families and conscience performance in our jobs, for example, we contribute to the good of the larger world around us (*CCC*, 1914). Beyond the personal sphere, we are called on to directly contribute to society, to build it up, by sharing our respective talents and abilities, and we owe loyalty to the communities we are a part of and respect for the authorities and laws that promote the common good (*CCC*, 1878-1880).

This duty includes taking part in public life, informing ourselves on public issues, and voting responsibly in light of the gospels and the teaching of the Church. We have a duty to speak out against inequity and to campaign for just laws or against unjust ones by writing to public officials, attending public meetings, or joining civic organizations. We have a duty to obey just laws, pay just taxes, and to defend our country if we are called upon (*CCC*, 2240).

It is important for societies to strike a balance between the common good and the rights of individuals. The individual man, woman, or child should never be regarded only as the means through which some perceived common goal is achieved (*CCC*, 1887). For example, a person must not be punished without due process of law on the grounds that this will serve some greater good. Whatever a society tries to do must conform to the standards of justice expressed in the Ten Commandments, in the gospels, and in Christian Tradition (*CCC*, 1888).

All people share natural dignity

"In view of the increasingly close ties of mutual dependence today between all the inhabitants and peoples of the earth, the apt pursuit and efficacious attainment of the universal common good now require of the community of nations that it organize itself in a manner suited to its present responsibilities, especially toward the many parts of the world which are still suffering from unbearable want.

To reach this goal, organizations of the international community, for their part, must make provision for men's different needs, both in the fields of social life—such as food supplies, health, education, labor and also in certain special circumstances which can crop up here and there, e.g., the need to promote the general improvement of developing countries, or to alleviate the distressing conditions in which refugees dispersed throughout the world find themselves, or also to assist migrants and their families."

Gaudium et Spes, 84 § 2

Individuals, too, must respect the dignity of every human person. "Attitudes of prejudice and bias against any individual for any reason, as well as actions or judgments based on prejudiced or biased views, violate God's will and law" (*USCCA*, p. 326). The Church has addressed this in strong terms, describing discrimination against or harassment of any person because of race, color, condition of life, or religion as "foreign to the mind of Christ" (*Nostra aetate*, 5). Nor is the obligation to respect others simply a matter of law or etiquette. "Social justice is both an attitude and a practical response based on the principle that everyone should look at another person as another self" (*USCCA*, p. 326).

Good order in human society requires that some people be invested with authority to keep the peace, protect life and property, provide for basic human needs, and govern institutions. This authority comes from God, and members of a society are obliged to respect it (*CCC*, 1897-1899, 1909-1910). At the same time, the members of a society have the right to decide who will exercise authority over them. However, since this authority does ultimately come from God, it is legitimate only so long as it is exercised in keeping with God's law. Citizens are not bound in conscience to obey unjust laws or to tolerate immoral actions by those in authority (*CCC*, 1901-1904).

The *Catechism* tells us that there are three conditions necessary for social justice: respect for the human person, for equality among people, and for human solidarity (*CCC*, 1943-1948). Social justice can be achieved only when we recognize the inherent rights of every person and realize that those rights flow from their dignity as human beings. Any authority that does not respect those rights has to depend on force in order to govern (1929-1931). "The duty of making oneself a neighbor to others and actively serving them becomes even more urgent when it involves the disadvantaged, in whatever area this may be" (*CCC*, 1932). "This same duty extends to those who think or act differently from us. The teaching of Christ goes so far as to require the forgiveness of offenses" (*CCC*, 1933), meaning that we must not hate our enemies as persons, even while we reject their thinking or behavior.

The differences among people–including their varying talents, aptitudes, and wealth–belong to God's plan, and they oblige us be generous with what God has given us. There are also differences, particularly in education and wealth, that do not come from God but from unjust human behavior. Any such behavior that affects basic human rights on the grounds of gender, race, color, language, or religion contradicts the gospel, and individuals and their governments share the obligation to oppose it (*CCC*, 1935, 1938). "Civil laws can partially help to eliminate fears, prejudices, and attitudes of pride and selfishness that cause injustice, but an inner spiritual conversion is also needed" (*USCCA*, p. 326).

Our natural tendency to interact with other people and live, not alone, but in community "serves as a moral foundation for an attitude of solidarity with each other and leads to a dedication to social justice for everyone" (*USCCA*, p. 325). God calls us to correct any sign or cause of injustices that undermine that solidarity. In the New Covenant, we are called to go beyond the requirements of the Old Law; we are called to live together in the spirit of the Beatitudes by experiencing God's love for us and returning that love both to God and our neighbor–and the term "neighbor" embraces the whole human community.

Sharing Questions

- What abuses of power have you observed or experienced yourself?
- How have you experienced solidarity in your workplace, town, or parish?
- Describe an occasion in which you spoke up about an abuse of power.

Living the Good News

Jesus emphasized the connection between faith and action, between what we believe and what we do. In that spirit, decide on an individual or group action that flows from what you have shared in this session. If you decide to act on your own, share your decision with the group. If you decide on a group action, determine among you whether individual members will take responsibility for various aspects of the action.

You are likely to benefit most from taking an action that arises from your own response to the session. However, you can consider one of the following suggestions or use these ideas to help develop one of your own:

- Become more active in civic life. For example, if you are not registered to vote, register. If you are not aware of local political issues, find out about them and consider how you might add to the discussion or offer solutions. Write to a local, state, or federal legislator who represents you, and express your opinion about a matter that affects the public good.

- Read "Communities of Salt and Light," which provides reflections on the social mission of the parish, and discuss it with your fellow parishioners and parish ministers. "Communities of Salt and Light" is available from the United States Conference of Catholic Bishops, 3211 4th Street NE, Washington, DC 20017-1194. Phone: 800-235-8722. The complete text is on the conference web site: www.usccb.org.

- Decide as a group how you can be in greater solidarity with a group that is oppressed. Pray for these people and begin to communicate with them in the spirit of sharing your common concerns.

- Consider and act on things you could do to promote solidarity in your workplace, town, or parish.

In light of this session, this week I commit to:

_____

_____

Lifting Our Hearts

Spend a few moments reflecting on segments of the human family that are set apart, marginalized, or subject to discrimination by those of us who see them as "different." Offer spontaneous prayers for the healing of these obstacles to human solidarity.

Pray together

Ever-present God,
you made all people in your image
by giving us judgment and freedom.

And yet you made us diverse
by giving us different talents,
different histories, and different points of view.

Help us to see in these differences
the unlimited potential of the life you have given us,
and help us to share and celebrate them
as the one family of the one God.

We ask this through Jesus Christ our Lord. Amen.

Looking Ahead

- Prepare for your next session by prayerfully reading and studying:
  - Session 6: Grace: The Life of God
  - Colossians 1:3-10
  - *The Collegeville Bible Commentary: New Testament* by Robert J. Karris, for insight into the passage from the Letter to the Colossians.
  - *United States Catholic Catechism for Adults*, Chapter 24 "Life in Christ – Part II: The Principles of the Christian Moral Life," on "God's law as our guide," "Grace and justification," and "The Church as mother and teacher," pp. 327-331.

- You may like consult the relevant paragraphs from the *Catechism of the Catholic Church*:
  - paragraphs 1949-1986 on the moral law
  - paragraphs 1987-2029 on grace and justification
  - paragraphs 2030-2051 on the Church as mother and teacher
- Remember to use RENEWING FAMILY FAITH and its helpful suggestions on how to extend the fruits of your sharing beyond your group, especially to your families (see page 114).

Grace: The Life of God

Suggested Environment

You may have a Bible and a candle on a small table, with the Bible opened to the Scripture text for this session. Display a picture of law enforcement personnel and one of Jesus as the Good Shepherd. Consider decorating the table with the color of the liturgical season.

It is helpful to have available the Catechism of the Catholic Church (CCC) *and the* United States Catholic Catechism for Adults (USCCA).

Lifting Our Hearts

Song Suggestion

"Amazing Grace," John Newton and John Rees

Prayer

Pray together

Lord Jesus Christ,
you promised to be among us
whenever we gather in your name.

We come together now
and ask you to stay with us always.

We are grateful for the gift of your Holy Spirit
dwelling within us.

Fill us with faith in you,
pour hope into our hearts
and help us to love you.

As we are caught up into the dynamism of your divine life,
Grant us a share in the energy and peace
of your eternal plan. Amen.

Sharing Our Good News

Before continuing, talk briefly about the results of your plan for Living the Good News *after the last session.*

Reflection 1

"I have 'nothing' to give you"

Pedro Arrupe set out to be a doctor, but he was distracted by a miracle. While he was studying medicine in his native Spain, he visited the shrine to the Blessed Virgin at Lourdes and saw a boy who had been disabled by polio get up from his chair and walk. Not long after that, Pedro Arrupe entered religious life. He was ordained a Jesuit priest in 1936, but not before he and all other Jesuits were expelled from Spain by the Spanish Republic. He served in Japan, where he was once accused of espionage and imprisoned, and he helped care for those injured when the atomic bomb was dropped on Hiroshima in 1945. He was superior general of the Jesuit order from 1965 to 1983, and traveled the world visiting Jesuit ministries. On one of these trips, after he had celebrated Mass in an impoverished Latin American village, Arrupe was approached by a local man whose appearance made the priest nervous. The man said he had something at home to give Father Arrupe. Reassured by a fellow priest, Father Arrupe went with the man to a house that was barely standing. "He had me sit on a rickety old chair," Father Arrupe remembered. "From there I could see the sunset. The big man said to me, 'Look, sir, how beautiful it is. . . . I didn't know how to thank you for all you have done for us. I have nothing to give you, but I thought you would like to see this sunset.'"

Sharing Question

• By worldly standards, the man described by Father Arrupe had nothing to give. Still, he was both moved and enabled by grace to share *something* of his life. When has someone been moved to share his or her life with you in a way that could not be measured by monetary value? When have you been moved to do that for another? How did you hear the voice of God on those occasions?

Grace helps us perfect the gift of freedom

The Examen of Consciousness is a spiritual practice described by St. Ignatius Loyola to reflect on the events of the day. The Examen, which should take about 15 minutes, is intended to open our hearts and minds more fully to God's will for us and to help us recognize the presence of God in everything we encounter.

The Examen, usually practiced once or twice each day, includes five steps:

1. Be aware of the presence of God. Ask the Holy Spirit to help you clearly recall and understand the events of this day.

2. Relive with gratitude the good things of this day–things you accomplished, things that were done for you or given to you, people you encountered and the ways in which you contributed to each other's lives, large and small things that made the day worthwhile.

3. Reflect on your emotions. Think about how you felt through the day–upbeat, pessimistic, compassionate, angry–and reflect on what God may be telling you through these feelings. Should you change your approach to some aspect of your life?

4. Pray about one particular part of this day. Ask the Holy Spirit to help you focus on an event, a feeling, a person–whether the experience was important or trivial, positive or negative. Reflect on and let your heart spontaneously thank God, ask God's help, or ask God's forgiveness.

5. Look forward to tomorrow. Ask God to help you with whatever may arise, and be aware of your emotions as you anticipate the new day. Pray from your response to these emotions, asking God for wisdom, patience, courage, hope.

Talk with Jesus in your heart, asking his forgiveness, protection, help, and guidance. Thank him for all he has done for you and for the world. End with the Lord's Prayer.

When we practice the Examen on a regular basis, we begin to notice patterns: patterns of God's grace, mercy and forgiveness; patterns of our response to God and others; patterns that reveal the roots of our failures as disciples of Jesus. The practice of the Examen of Consciousness both raises our awareness of God's great love for us and prepares us for the celebration of the Sacrament of Penance and Reconciliation.

You can learn more by clicking on The Daily Examen at http://ignatianspirituality.com/

The moral law comes from God. It teaches us the way of living that leads to the peace and happiness God promises. It also teaches us to avoid any behavior that turns us away from God (*CCC*, 1950). As we discussed in Session 3, we have a lifelong obligation to form our conscience by learning God's law and to follow an informed conscience when we make the many moral choices life presents. There are several interrelated expressions of the moral law, including the natural law, revealed law, and civil laws (*CCC*, 1952).

Our teachers in faith have often explained the natural law as written in the conscience of every human being. This means that God created us with the ability to determine by reason what is morally right and what is morally wrong, as we have discussed in previous sessions. The main principles of the natural law are expressed in the Ten Commandments (*CCC*, 1954-1955).

The unchanging natural law is the foundation for our rights and responsibilities as free men and women. As a result, a basic agreement about ethical principles, such as respect for each other's lives, property, and reputation, arises naturally whenever people experience themselves, and interact with each other, as rational human beings. These basic moral values are articulated by various religious traditions and are commonly accepted by the entire human family. They are essential to our ability to live together in society and are the basis for our civil law (*CCC*, 1952-1954, 1959). When civil law contradicts natural law–as it does, for example, when it permits the abortion of unborn children–it is not the natural law that has changed but the civil law that has become detached from the truth (*CCC*, 1956).

The term "revealed law" refers to the law of God as it is proclaimed and illuminated in the Bible, first of all in the Old Testament. There we read that God revealed his law to Israel through Moses, a law that "expresses many truths naturally accessible to reason" (*CCC*, 1961)–the natural law put into words and summed up in the Ten Commandments. This law prohibits whatever is contrary to the love of God and neighbor, and it requires whatever is essential to that love (*CCC*, 1961-1962). Our Christian tradition holds that the law revealed to Moses, while it is holy and unchanging, was a first step in God's plan to save all people from the consequences of sin and to draw all people into union with him through Jesus (*CCC*, 1963).

The Old Testament, including the Law of Moses, looked ahead to the New Law expressed in the gospels and particularly in the standards for living that Jesus preached in the Sermon on the Mount. The New Law does more than warn against sin. Made alive by the Holy Spirit, it tells us how to live together in charity and it helps us do so by the grace we receive in the sacraments (*CCC*, 1965-1966). It makes clear what the *Catechism* calls a "surprising" characteristic of the Reign of God, that it is open to everyone who embraces the law–"the poor, the humble, the afflicted, the pure of heart" (*CCC*, 1967) and those persecuted for their faith in Christ. The New Law challenges us to more than a legalistic obedience; it requires us to decide between two ways of living. "The entire Law of the Gospel is contained in the *'new commandment'* of Jesus, to love one another as he has loved us" (Cf. *Jn* 15:12; 13:34) (*CCC*, 1970).

Sharing Question

• In what way is your response to God's law different from your response to civil law? In what way is it similar?

Pondering the Word

Grace: God's amazing gift to us

Colossians 1:3-10

Sharing Questions

• Take a moment to reflect on what word, phrase, or image from the Scripture passage touches your heart or speaks to your life. Reflect on this in silence, or share it aloud.

• St. Paul writes of the gospel "bearing fruit and growing" in the hearts of Christians–implying that the faithful are "works in progress." In what ways do you feel you have grown over time in your understanding of the gospel and what it asks of you?

Reflection 2

"I was blind, but now I see"

"Amazing Grace," written by John Newton in 1779, is one of the most recognizable songs in the English language. A collection in the Library of Congress includes more than 3,000 recordings of the hymn in styles ranging from gospel to rap. "Amazing grace," wrote Newton, a clergyman who had been a foul-mouthed, immoral seaman in the slave trade. "How sweet the sound that saved a wretch like me. I once was lost and now am found, was blind but now I see." The appeal of his lyric no doubt is in its message of redemption. Grace enables us to experience God's favor and forgiveness, God's power and his presence in our lives and in the world. Grace is warmly personal: Each of us has been saved and set free; each of us has been found and given new sight by God and God alone. The "amazing" reality is that, by God's generosity and goodness, we have been given a share in the divine nature, in the very being and life of God (*2 Pt* 1:4). That gift is grace, and it is through grace that we are "justified"–that is, cleansed of our sins and restored to friendship with God by the action of the Holy Spirit (*CCC*, 1987-1988).

Spotlight on the *Catechism*

"In this recognition of the reality and important role of grace in the Christian moral life, we face a struggle prompted by our culture's understanding that everything is within our human power. 'My power is sufficient.' Compare this with our understanding that we are indeed blessed and gifted, but much of what we fight to achieve–while written in our hearts–still needs God's grace because of the presence of sin and our inherent human weakness. The New Law is truly Good News, for not only does God give us the moral law that leads us to salvation, but through grace we receive divine assistance to follow it. . . . "

United States Catholic Catechism for Adults, pp. 329-330

Grace is the help that God gives us–freely and on his own initiative–to answer his call to an intimate relationship with the Holy Trinity and to the eternal life made possible by the sacrifice and resurrection of Jesus (*CCC*, 1996-1997, 1999). Traditionally, the Church has spoken of *actual* grace and *sanctifying* grace. Actual grace refers to moments when God intervenes in our lives to initiate or develop our growth in holiness– for example, when we feel moved to perform an act of charity or when we restrain ourselves from making a harsh comment. Sanctifying grace refers to a lasting state of friendship with God and embrace of his will, a gift we can accept with our free will by turning toward God and away from anything that contradicts his law. When (with God's help) we have made that choice, God enables us in our attitudes, words, and actions, to live out his love in our daily lives. We participate in the life of God, who is present within us and directs us toward peace, justice, and reconciliation (*CCC*, 2000, 2002).

The Spirit makes a gift of grace whenever we receive any of the sacraments (*CCC*, 2003). We first receive grace and justification in Baptism, when God, as the liturgy says, welcomes us into his holy people–when we become members of the Church (*CCC*, 1992). As we mature, the Holy Spirit first moves us to repentance in which we not only receive forgiveness but experience an inner renewal, a change of heart (*CCC*, 1989). We are freed from attachment to sin, and we accept God's justice and submit ourselves again to his will (*CCC*, 1990-1991).

Grace enables us to leave behind any prejudices and selfishness. Grace gives us the strength to "die to ourselves" or "lay down our lives" in making the difficult choices that will have positive effects on others and on society. All Christians have a responsibility to spread the good news of God's grace living within them–as St. Paul wrote in our reading for this session, to "lead lives worthy of the Lord, fully pleasing to him" (*Col* 1:10), bearing fruit in good works and growing in our knowledge of God. By word and example, we invite others to learn and to share in the gifts of God's unconditional love for all (*CCC*, 2003-2004).

When we answer the call to lead a Christian life, we do it in the Church in communion with all the baptized, sharing the grace of the Eucharist, the "source and summit of the Christian life" (*LG*, 11) (*CCC*, 1324). From the Church, we receive the word of God in the gospels–specifically, in the teaching of Jesus; we receive grace in the sacraments; we benefit from the examples of holiness provided by the Virgin Mary and all the saints, and by those who follow those examples today (*CCC*, 2030).

The Church, beginning with the apostles, has been entrusted by Jesus with the interpretation of his teaching to guide us in our lives as individuals and as societies (*CCC*, 2032). This teaching authority– known as the *magisterium*–is a sacred trust that the Church carries out with the guidance of the Holy Spirit. The Church exercises this authority by safeguarding and handing down the teaching of Jesus. In passing down the faith and in moral teaching that flows from the gospels and from Divine Tradition, the call of the *magisterium* is to bring together in unity the members of the Body with Christ, its Head. The Church transmits the articles of faith and interprets moral law as a *service* to the people of God. In this, the Church imitates Christ, her Head, who came into the world to serve.

The Church carries out these responsibilities largely through religious education of children and adults and through preaching.

This moral teaching–summed up in the Beatitudes and in the "great commandment" to love God and neighbor–relies heavily on the Creed, the Lord's Prayer, and the Ten Commandments (*CCC*, 2033). The pope and the bishops in particular, as successors to the apostles, have received the primary authority to teach us what to believe–the faith, how to live–the life of charity, and what to hope for–eternal life with God (*CCC*, 2034-2035). The Church has also established precepts, such as the obligation to attend Sunday Mass and receive the Eucharist during Eastertide, that are designed to promote an active spiritual, moral, and liturgical life. We members of the Church have a *right* to receive these teachings and an *obligation* to apply them to our lives (*CCC*, 2037).

Sharing Question

• How do you understand grace to be present in your life?

• Recall and share a time when have you felt that, through actual grace, God was prompting you to do a specific good or avoid a specific evil.

• Recall and share a graced moment you have shared with your family or friends.

Living the Good News

Jesus emphasized the connection between faith and action, between what we believe and what we do. In that spirit, decide on an individual or group action that flows from what you have shared in this session. If you decide to act on your own, share your decision with the group. If you decide on a group action, determine among you whether individual members will take responsibility for various aspects of the action.

You are likely to benefit most from taking an action that arises from your own response to the session. However, you can consider one of the following suggestions or use these ideas to help develop one of your own:

• Ask God for insight into attitudes you may have that obstruct the action of grace in your life.

• Practice the The Examen of Consciousness, which is described in this session, to review your day in light of God's presence and his will for you. You can learn more by clicking on The Examen at http://ignatianspirituality.com/

• Read and reflect on *Veritatis Splendor,* an encyclical letter of Pope John Paul II, available at book stores, at www.usccb.org, and at www.vatican.va. Write journal entries about the ideas in this letter that are significant to you. Share them with another person.

In light of this session, this week I commit to:

_____

_____

Lifting Our Hearts

Take a few moments to consider ways in which God's grace has touched you–either by helping you to decide how to act in a specific situation or by helping you to maintain a sustained friendship with God. Offer spontaneous prayers of thanksgiving for these gifts.

Leader	Let us pray silently that the Spirit of God will inspire and encourage us to know and to accomplish the work of the Lord Jesus in our daily lives through grace.

Prayed by alternating groups or by groups on opposite sides of the room:

Group 1	My spirit hungers for your love, O Divine Lover of hearts. I long for your presence and the joy of your peace.
Group 2	Teach us what it means to love, O God. Show us all that love includes, love of self, love of others, love of all the earth, love of all that you yourself love.
Group 1	Teach us that all of your creation is sacred and that you love all that you have made. Remind us often that to love a neighbor is just another way of loving you.
Group 2	Bless all those we love, O God, and help us to love all those you love – the poor, the homeless, the distressed, those different from ourselves.
Group 1	Awaken us to the present moment to see the suffering around us. By your grace, move our hearts to reach out to those in pain.

Group 2   Inspire us to serve them, Lord.
              Let our love extend in kindness.
              Love those we love, dear God,
              and help us to love those you love.

All   **Love all those we love, dear God, and help us to love
              all those you love. Amen.**

Looking Ahead

- Prepare for your next session by prayerfully reading and studying:

    - Session 7: Total Commitment to God

    - Matthew: 19:16-21 (The encounter between Jesus and the rich young man)

    - *The Collegeville Bible Commentary: New Testament* by Robert J. Karris, for insight into the passage from the Gospel of Matthew.

    - *United States Catholic Catechism for Adults*, summary of doctrinal statements for the first commandment, pp. 347-348; for the second commandment, p. 358; and for the third commandment, pp. 369-370.

- You may also like to consult the relevant chapters from the *United States Catechism for Adults*:

    - Chapter 25 "The First Commandment: Believe in the True God"

    - Chapter 26 "The Second Commandment: Reverence God's Name"

    - Chapter 27 "The Third Commandment: Love the Lord's Day"

- You may also like to consult the relevant paragraphs in the *Catechism of the Catholic Church*:

    - paragraphs 2052-2082 on the Ten Commandments

    - paragraphs 2083-2141 on the first commandment

    - paragraphs 2142-2167 on the second commandment

    - paragraphs 2168-2195 on the third commandment

- Remember to use RENEWING FAMILY FAITH and its helpful suggestions on how to extend the fruits of your sharing beyond your group, especially to your families (see page 114).

Total Commitment to God

The first three commandments

Suggested Environment

You may have a Bible and a candle on a small table, with the Bible opened to the Scripture text for this session. Display an image representative of the Ten Commandments and/or pictures or examples of "other gods" in our lives (car keys, money, a "hand-held device.") Consider decorating the table with the color of the liturgical season.

It is helpful to have available the Catechism of the Catholic Church (CCC) *and the* United States Catholic Catechism for Adults (USCCA).

Lifting Our Hearts

Song Suggestion

"Center of My Life," Paul Inwood

Prayer

Invite three members of the group to read in turn the three verses:

Leader   It is difficult today, dear God, to be faithful to your commands. Implant deep within us a desire to follow your way of love and truth.

All   **Lord Jesus, set us ablaze with faith.**
Anchor us in fidelity to your commandments.

Reader 1   O God, you are the center of our lives.
Give us the grace always to place you
    first in our lives.
Help us to put our trust in you
and be authentic followers of your word.

All	**Lord Jesus, set us ablaze with faith.**
	Anchor us in fidelity to your commandments.

Reader 2   Oh God, our Creator, your name is holy.
May our lips and our lives proclaim the sacredness
of your presence.
Let us revere you in all creation.
Forgive us for the times we take your name in vain
or slander one another.

All   **Lord Jesus, set us ablaze with faith.**
Anchor us in fidelity to your commandments.

Reader 3   Oh God, our companion, you are Lord of the Sabbath.
Help us to keep Sunday holy,
participating fully in the celebration of the Eucharist,
and giving witness to our communion with our lives.

All   **Come Holy Spirit, enter into our gathering space.**
Fill us with renewed faith and a fiery zeal
to live committed and heroic lives.
May our hearts burn with love for you, your law,
for life, for justice, and for peace. Amen.

Sharing Our Good News

Before continuing, talk briefly about the results of your plan for Living the Good News *after the last session.*

Reflection 1

Honoring God and each other

Catherine de Hueck Doherty made a long journey from her privileged childhood in imperial Russia to her simple existence in the woods of Ontario. And yet she hadn't traveled far from her roots–specifically from the lessons she learned from her wealthy mother, who served the poor as a way of serving God. Raised in the Russian Orthodox Church, Catherine converted to Catholicism after the Bolshevik revolution drove her family from their homeland. Convinced that only the gospel–and certainly not Bolshevism–could bring true justice and peace to the world, she sold her belongings and assumed a life of prayer and service to the poor. She moved to the slums of Toronto, and in 1931 she established "Friendship House" where she

and a few people of like mind provided food, clothes, and shelter
to those in need. This began a missionary movement that spread to
other cities. Catherine married American journalist Eddie Doherty,
and they moved to Combermere, Ontario. At their home, Madonna
House, they set up a training center for lay ministry. Although they
remained laity, the couple professed simple vows of poverty, chastity,
and obedience. People from around the world visited Madonna House,
and other centers were established; seventeen were still operating in
the 21st century. A woman of deep spirituality, Catherine was also a
counselor and a prolific writer. "Catherine's life illustrates the First
Commandment in that she lived her life loving the Lord with all her
heart, soul, and mind above all else and because of that, respected and
worked for the dignity of every human being" (USCCA, p. 341).

Sharing Questions

• How does Catherine de Hueck and Eddie Doherty's total
  commitment to God inspire you in your own life?

Following Jesus means keeping the Ten Commandments (CCC,
2053), but it means a great deal more. As we have already seen,
the commandments in their entirety are an expression of the natural
law that God implants in the heart of every human being; the
commandments put into plain language the essential duties of human
beings as well as their fundamental rights (CCC, 2070-2071). As Jesus
taught us, these commandments, handed down by God through
Moses, were not abolished by the New Covenant, but their full
meaning has been revealed in the Gospel, especially in the Beatitudes
and in the Great Commandment to love God and neighbor. The
author of Matthew's Gospel shows how explicitly Jesus expressed
this transformation of the Commandments: "Do not think that I have
come to abolish the law or the prophets; I have come not to abolish
but to fulfill. For truly I tell you, until heaven and earth pass away, not
one letter, not one stroke of a letter, will pass from the law until all is
accomplished. . . . You have heard that it was said, 'You shall love your
neighbor and hate your enemy.' But I say to you, Love your enemies
and pray for those who persecute you, so that you may be children of
your Father in heaven . . . " (Mt 5:17-18,43-45). In every case, Jesus took
the commandments to a radically different level.

The commandments, as they have been expressed in Christian
tradition, are succinct–even blunt–but we should not think of them
even in their original form only as a list of orders designed to keep

Spotlight on the *Catechism*

"Our surrounding culture is filled with many distractions that shut out the majestic voice of our holy and glorious God. St. Augustine, commenting on his troubled youth, speaks of this experience with these words, 'You were with me, but I was not with you. Created things kept me from you; yet if they had not been in you they would not have been at all.' But God was not simply a passive presence to Augustine, a diffident lover wondering what to do. Augustine tells us that God spoke with a vigorous voice: 'You called, you shouted, and you broke through my deafness. You breathed your fragrance on me. . . . I have tasted you, now I hunger and thirst for more' (*The Confessions*, bk. 10, no. 27).

This is the best context for appreciating the importance of the First Commandment. As God did with Augustine, he does for us again – calling, shouting, trying to break through our deafness, breathing his fragrance upon us."

United States Catholic Catechism for Adults, p. 346

us in line. On the contrary, the commandments were presented to the Hebrew people–whom God had just delivered from slavery in Egypt–in the context of freedom. "If you obey the commandments of the Lord your God that I am commanding you today," Moses told the Hebrews, "by loving the Lord your God, walking in his ways, and observing his commandments, decrees, and ordinances, then you shall live and become numerous" (*Dt* 30:16).

God gave the commandments in connection with the covenant he was making with his people; in fact, God proposed the covenant–demonstrated and expressed his love for his people–*before* he gave the commandments (*CCC*, 2060-2061). What the commandments added to the covenant was the expectation that men and women would lead moral lives, in harmony with God and neighbor, in thanksgiving for the love that God had first shown for them (*CCC*, 2062). So the commandments are not about crime and punishment; they are about love.

The Ten Commandments given to the Hebrews–with the implication of love for God and neighbor–have remained central to the teaching of the Church (*CCC*, 2064-2066, 2068). The first three commandments concern love of God, and the other seven concern love of neighbor; however, the commandments have a certain unity, because to violate one is to violate all. "One cannot honor another person without blessing God his Creator. One cannot adore God without loving all . . . his creatures" (*CCC*, 2069).

Sharing Question

- Share an experience that made you aware that the commandments were not only written in Scripture but implanted in your heart?

Pondering the Word

"Then come, follow me"

Matthew 19:16-21

Sharing Questions

- Take a moment to reflect on what word, phrase, or image from the Scripture passage touches your heart or speaks to your life. Reflect on this in silence, or share it aloud.

- Jesus makes the same invitation to us as he did to the young man in the gospel story. How can we respond to Jesus within the vocation we have chosen?

Reflection 2

"You shall have no other gods"

"I am the Lord, your God, . . you shall have no other gods besides me" (Exodus 20:2-3).

The *Catechism* points out that the first commandment embraces the virtues we talked about in our fourth session: faith, hope, and charity (*CCC*, 2086).

With *faith*, we believe in God, we accept his words, and we live according to his will. We reject anything that threatens or contradicts our faith (*CCC*, 2087-2089). With *hope*, we depend on God's grace to help us return his love and live by his commandments with the expectation of a life forever in his presence. We do not stop believing in God's promise of salvation or in his forgiveness, nor do we think we can save ourselves without God's grace or obtain forgiveness without repentance (*CCC*, 2090-2092). With *charity*, we wholeheartedly return God's love by loving him and by loving everything he has created (*CCC*, 2093), and that includes caring for those who are in need and actively protecting the environment.

Spotlight on the *Catechism*

"A name in some way conveys the reality of a person–the origin, the history, the very being of the person. That is why people are protective about their names and expect them to be treated with honor. The name of God obviously deserves the highest honor and respect. The Lord gives us a Commandment that asks us to reverence his name and not to use it in a disrespectful or manipulative way. When Jesus taught the Our Father, his first petition was 'Hallowed be thy name.' We also praise God's holy name in every Mass at the beginning of the Eucharistic Prayer when we recite or sing the Holy, Holy, Holy."

United States Catholic Catechism for Adults, p. 354

The first commandment calls us to adore God, which we do in prayer, and not anyone or anything else. That means that we don't become so self-absorbed that we are, in our own minds, more important than God. It also means that we don't allow any other person, or object, or goal, or desire, or possession, or pastime to take the place of God at the center of our lives (*CCC*, 2096-2098, 2113). While the commandment literally refers to "other gods"– meaning religious idols–it also can refer to such things as food, drink, gambling, wealth, or political power when those things become central in a person's life. Jesus could not have been more clear: "No one can serve two masters" (*Mt* 6:24).

Another implication of this commandment is that every person is "bound to seek the truth, especially in what concerns God and his Church, and to embrace it and hold on to it as they come to know it" (DH 1 § 2) (*CCC*, 2104). At the same time, Christians who study and cherish their own faith also have a duty to respect those who practice other religions. "The Catholic Church rejects nothing that is true and holy in these religions. She regards with sincere reverence those ways of conduct and of life, those precepts and teachings which, though differing in many aspects from the ones she holds and sets forth, nonetheless often reflect a ray of that Truth which enlightens all men" (*Nostra aetate*, 2). Still, we Catholics are to expose the rest of the world to our faith through the example of our own lives and through the impact we have on the "mores, laws, and structures" (AA, 13 § 1) of our communities (*CCC*, 2105).

"You shall not make wrongful use of the name of the Lord your God" (Exodus 20:7).

The second commandment calls on us, specifically, to respect the name of God and any term that refers to God, and the commandment generally requires us to be respectful when we're speaking about religious matters (CCC, 2142). That means that we should avoid any improper use of the names of God, of Jesus, of the Virgin Mary, and of any of the saints (CCC, 2146). This commandment also forbids false oaths in God's name–either promising to do something one has no intention of doing or lying, for example, while testifying under oath (CCC, 2150-2152).

"Remember the sabbath day, and keep it holy" (Exodus 20:10).

One of the concrete ways that we Catholics keep the Sabbath holy, as the third commandment requires, is by gathering as parish communities to celebrate the Eucharist. In fact, the Eucharistic celebration on the Lord's Day of the sacrifice and resurrection of Jesus is at the heart of the Church's life. When we gather on Saturday evening or on Sunday to celebrate the Eucharist, we fulfill a moral obligation to give visible, public, and regular worship to God (CCC, 2176-2177). Participating at Mass with other members of the Church also gives witness to our union with each other and with the Holy Trinity (CCC, 2182).

The third commandment also requires us to consider how we spend our time. Setting aside Sunday as the Lord's Day helps us enjoy adequate time for rest and leisure and for cultivation of our cultural, social, and especially our family and religious lives. It is also an especially appropriate day for visiting the sick or those who spend much of their week alone (CCC, 2180-2184). The commandment tells us to avoid unnecessary work or other activities that will prevent us from setting aside Sunday in this way. While there may occasionally be reasons why a person cannot worship and rest on Sunday, "The faithful should see to it that legitimate excuses do not lead to habits prejudicial to religion, family life, and health" (CCC, 2185). By keeping the Lord's Day in all these ways, we are responding to the commandment that Jesus said was the first and greatest of all: "You shall love the Lord your God with all your heart, and with all your soul, and with all your mind" (Mt 22:37). The call to observe the Sabbath is a call to make that radical choice of God before anything else in our lives.

Sharing Questions

• How is God number one in your life?

• The second commandment tells us not to take the Lord's name in vain. What does that mean in today's world?

• How do you observe the Lord's Day?

Living the Good News

Jesus emphasized the connection between faith and action, between what we believe and what we do. In that spirit, decide on an individual or group action that flows from what you have shared in this session. If you decide to act on your own, share your decision with the group. If you decide on a group action, determine among you whether individual members will take responsibility for various aspects of the action.

You are likely to benefit most from taking an action that arises from your own response to the session. However, you can consider one of the following suggestions or use these ideas to help develop one of your own:

- Pray for an increase in faith for yourself and one other person.
- Take a more active part in Sunday Eucharist by becoming a lector, Eucharistic minister, or greeter.
- If you have the habit of using God's name in a careless manner, ask someone to call your attention to it so that you can eliminate it.
- Think through how you spend your Sundays. Set aside some time for prayer, rest, and acts of kindness for someone in need.

In light of this session, this week I commit to:

_____

_____

Lifting Our Hearts

Christians call on God in prayer using many names such as Ever-living God, Creator and Redeemer, Lord Almighty. Take a few moments to reflect on the names you have used to speak to God. Speak the names spontaneously. To each name, the whole group can respond: "We praise your name."

After a few minutes, pray together:

Glory to God in the highest,
and on earth peace to people
  of good will.
We praise you,
we bless you,
we adore you,
we glorify you,
we give you thanks for your
  great glory,

Lord God, heavenly King,
O God, almighty Father.

Lord Jesus Christ, Only Begotten Son,
Lord God, Lamb of God, Son of
    the Father,
you take away the sins of the world,
    have mercy on us;
you take away the sins of the world,
    receive our prayer;
you are seated at the right hand of
    the father,
        have mercy on us.

For you alone are the Holy One,
you alone are the Lord,
you alone are the Most High,
Jesus Christ,
with the Holy Spirit,
in the glory of God the Father.
Amen.

The Roman Missal

Looking Ahead

- Prepare for your next session by prayerfully reading and studying:

    - Session 8: The Family: The Domestic Church

    - Luke 2:41-52 (the child Jesus in the temple)

    - *The Collegeville Bible Commentary: New Testament*
      by Robert J. Karris, for insight into the passage
      from the Gospel of Luke

    - The summary of doctrinal statements regarding the
      fourth commandment, presented in the *United States
      Catholic Catechism for Adults*, pp. 382-383

- You may also like to consult the *United States Catholic
  Catechism for Adults*, Chapter 28 "The Fourth Commandment:
  Strengthen Your Family."

- You may also like to consult the *Catechism of the Catholic Church*,
  paragraphs 2196-2257 on the fourth commandment.

- Remember to use RENEWING FAMILY FAITH and its helpful suggestions
  on how to extend the fruits of your sharing beyond your group,
  especially to your families (see page 114).

The Family: The Domestic Church

The fourth commandment

Suggested Environment

You may have a Bible and a candle on a small table, with the Bible opened to the Scripture text for this session. Display pictures of families, especially those including grandparents and others who have helped pass on the faith to younger generations. Consider decorating the table with the color of the liturgical season.

It is helpful to have available the Catechism of the Catholic Church (CCC) *and the* United States Catholic Catechism for Adults (USCCA).

Lifting Our Hearts

Song Suggestion

"Where Charity and Love Prevail," Paul Benoit, OSB

Prayer

Pray together

Most Holy Trinity,
as we gather in this Christian community,
we feel the ties that bind us together with you.

Help us to imitate your example of unity
as we live in our families, in our communities,
and in the Church.

Help us to use authority with justice and compassion.
Help us to accept authority with faithfulness and humility.
Help us to freely assist those who need our assistance
and graciously accept the assistance of those who offer it to us.

Strengthen the ties of our human family
as we look forward to the perfect unity
of life forever with you and your saints.
Amen.

Sharing Our Good News

Before continuing, talk briefly about the results of your plan for Living the
Good News *after the last session.*

Reflection 1

Family life as mission

Greg and Kate Kremer went out of their way to enrich the faith
formation of their children – in fact, they went to Central America.

Greg is special assistant to the executive director of RENEW
International, involved in the marketing and promotion of RENEW's
services.

He and Kate have always focused their energy on how to make a
difference in the world. "This is still true," he said, "but far more
important to me is how to help form my children so that they will be
able to make a difference and understand why they are doing it."

Feeling spiritually drained by "the crazy schedule of events that
having three children seems to generate," Greg said, the Kremers
decided that their family "needed to step out of our comfort zones
. . . to create a life-changing experience that would provide an
opportunity to talk about our faith in a meaningful way with our kids
– and maybe even encounter Christ."

So the Kremers, who knew from Scripture that Jesus could be found
in a special way among the poor, took their children to work for
two weeks at Nuestros Pequeños Hermanos–Our Little Children–a
Catholic orphanage in Nicaragua.

It was an eye-opening, faith-enriching experience in many ways,
but Greg was particularly struck by what occurred while the family
attended an evening praise service:

"I was standing in the back of a crowd of 150 kids with my arms
around my son Jacob. I noticed that a dozen or so of the kids were
turned around looking at us rather than at the speaker.

"I asked Jacob why he thought they were staring at us. He was quiet for a moment, then said, 'Probably because they wish they had a dad to hold them too.'

"Tears welled up in my eyes as I said, 'That's Jesus looking at us.' "

The children at the orphanage have healthy meals, decent shelter, a basic education, and adult compassion and support.

"But the one thing they don't have that every kid longs for," Greg said, "is a solid family – parents to love and hold them. I was so pleased that my kids could see this, and I knew that their hearts would expand because of it. . . .

"It was a life-changing trip that helped us understand how wealthy we are in terms of resources and family, and I am certain that it will help all of us take our faith out of church and into the world for years to come."

Sharing Question

• Can you share a story about you and your family encountering Jesus in others? What opportunities are there for you to have that experience?

"Honor your father and your mother . . . ." (Exodus 20:12).

Although the fourth commandment refers specifically only to love of father and mother, it is an expression of the communion of all people–the whole human family–for which our model is the Holy Trinity–three Persons in one divine nature, bound together by love. The first three commandments deal with the love of God. The other seven are about love of neighbor, which means love of *everyone*. This fourth commandment teaches us how we are to apply the model of the Trinity to our relationships with members of our families and with others who have legitimate authority over us or who are under our authority. The commandment is addressed to children and adults alike, to parents and siblings, because it expresses the kind of relationships all family members are to have with one another (CCC, 2197-2199). Further, "it extends to the duties of pupils to teachers, employees to employers, subordinates to leaders, citizens to their country, and to those who administer or govern it" (CCC, 2199).

The fact that the fourth commandment refers directly to the family reflects the important part the family, as the most basic social unit, plays within the other large and small societies we live in–our neighborhoods, our towns, our country. The Christian family has often been referred to as a "domestic church." This means that a family–an image of the unity of the Holy Trinity–is a communion of two or more persons, a community committed to prayer and charity (*CCC*, 2204-2005).

According to the Book of Genesis, God instituted the family at the same time that he created human beings. Furthermore, God confirmed the central place of the family when he himself took on human form, in the person of Jesus, within the context of the Holy Family. The gospels imply that Jesus spent the first 30 years or so of his life in a family environment and, during that time, learned about love, commitment, and mutual respect.

Family can take many forms–for example, husband, wife, and children; a single parent and children; spouses and their children from previous marriages; a single person with extended ties through parents and siblings. Whatever the circumstances, the commandment calls family members to live in harmony, justice, and love. Perhaps the greatest love is experienced in family relationships and the greatest pain when vows are broken and love fades. "The relationships within the family bring an affinity of feelings, affections and interests, arising above all from the members' respect for one another" (*CCC*, 2206).

In their pastoral message *Follow the Way of Love*, the Catholic bishops of the United States pointed out four "challenges" presented by family life–living faithfully, giving life, growing in mutuality, and taking time. These are "challenges," the bishops said, because they represent ideals and goals that are often in conflict with a culture that thrives on self-indulgence and instant gratification.

The sacrament of marriage calls a man and woman to be *faithful* to God as God

Anyone who needs me is my neighbor

"The parable of the Good Samaritan (cf. *Lk* 10:25-37) offers two particularly important clarifications. Until that time, the concept of 'neighbor' was understood as referring essentially to one's countrymen and to foreigners who had settled in the land of Israel; in other words, to the closely-knit community of a single country or people. This limit is now abolished. Anyone who needs me, and whom I can help, is my neighbor. The concept of 'neighbor' is now universalized, yet it remains concrete. Despite being extended to all mankind, it is not reduced to a generic, abstract and undemanding expression of love, but calls for my own practical commitment here and now."

Pope Benedict XVI, *Deus caritas est*, 1§15

is faithful to them. They are called to live every day in light of their promise to be bound together in love "in good times or in bad, for better or worse, in sickness and in health." The sacrament calls a couple to welcome new *life* in the form of their children and also to open their hearts and extend their hands to embrace and help sustain the larger family in the parish and in the wider community—and teach their children by example to do the same.

Spouses are also called to live in a partnership—a *mutuality*—in which as individuals and as a couple they share dreams and plans and contribute their respective knowledge and talents to work toward their goals. Theirs is a relationship of mutual need and mutual respect and is therefore a model for their relationships with their larger family and the community at large.

Finally, the married couple is called to give to each other and their children the elusive but precious gift of *time*. The intimacy between husband and wife depends on this gift. So do the security and trust and education of their children. Giving this gift may run headlong into the obstacles of long work days; civic, social and recreational activities; and the many demands of feeding a family and maintaining a home. That's what makes it a gift—the determination that it is most important and the decision to make the time not only to be with each other but for the whole family to be with God in prayer at home and at the Sunday Eucharist.

Sharing Question

• How was your faith nurtured in the family? How were your attitudes and values formed?

Pondering the Word

Mary treasured these things in her heart

Luke 2:41-52

Sharing Questions

• Take a moment to reflect on what word, phrase, or image from the Scripture passage touches your heart or speaks to your life. Reflect on this in silence, or share it aloud.

• What does this say to us about family life?

Reflection 2

Family love and duty

The gospel passage we just read is the only description we have of a personal interchange involving the three members of the Holy Family. In this episode, we see the dynamics we might expect– parents worrying about their child and questioning his behavior; a maturing boy, excited about his growing knowledge and testing the limits of independence, and ultimately, a family bound together by mutual love and respect. Of course, this family was unique, the portal through which the Savior entered the world and the sanctuary in which he prepared for his ministry. Still, this family is our model. What we learn within our own families about authority, stability, and relationships is often what we live in the wider world, and what we do in our families often has an impact far beyond our homes. "The family is the community in which, from childhood, one can learn moral values, begin to honor God, and make good use of freedom. Family life is an initiation into life in society" (CCC, 2207).

The members of a family should take care of those among them who are young, ill, or in material need. To the extent that a family cannot do this, the responsibility falls to other individuals, families, or social organizations, including the church, and ultimately to society itself. At the root of this responsibility is the need to protect the institution of the family which is essential to a peaceful and just society (CCC, 2207-2210).

The specific words of the fourth commandment concern the honor, born of natural affection and gratitude, that children owe to the parents who gave them life, love them, and work to support and educate them (CCC, 2214-2215). This honor is expressed in obedience while a child is dependent on parents, and in respect when a child has become an independent adult (CCC, 2214-2217).

The commandment also reminds adult children of their responsibilities to provide as much material help and moral support as possible when parents are old, ill, lonely, or in any kind of distress (CCC, 2218). This implication of the commandment has become more meaningful than ever as more people live into their eighties and nineties and beyond.

The obligations implied by the fourth commandment do not flow only from the bottom up. Just as children have duties toward their parents, parents have responsibilities toward their children, and siblings to each other. Children also "should work to reduce rivalries, angers, hurts, and hostilities among brothers and sisters" (*USCCA*, p. 377). Besides keeping their children safe and healthy in mind and body, parents are the first teachers of their daughters and sons. Parents teach by creating a home characterized by tenderness, forgiveness, respect, faithfulness, and unselfishness. Parents also teach by their own example of moderation, good judgment, and humility (*CCC*, 2223). As the baptism ritual reminds us, parents are also the "first teachers of their children in the ways of faith." "Parents should teach their children to pray by praying with them from their earliest years. Parents . . . must also ensure their children's Catholic religious education and regular participation in Mass and other aspects of parish life" (*USCCA*, p. 378).

The fourth commandment reaches beyond the natural family and applies to the relationships between those in authority and those whom they govern. This is true with respect to employees and employers, to students and teachers, and to citizens and governments. In all such relationships, authority should be exercised only for the common good and should never impose anything at odds with the dignity of human beings or the natural law (*CCC*, 2235). Governments must grant political rights

We are called by Jesus to welcome everyone

"One of the constant features of American history is the fact of immigration and the process of conversion whereby the receiving population learns to soften its heart and open its arms to welcome the newcomer. As we have seen with the earlier waves of Irish, German, Italian and Eastern European immigrants, this process takes time—time for the immigrants to assimilate and time for the receiving population to become comfortable with the newcomers. . . .

One of the most distinguishing features of the Catholic Church is that we are called to be 'universal' in fact as well as in name. This means that there must be no dividing lines within our parishes, no second-class parishioners—all are welcome, without exception. In many instances, this will require a process of conversion within our own hearts as well as within our parish communities. I know that it sometimes takes time to adjust when encountering a new group of people, but it is precisely to this that Jesus calls us, one and all."

Most Rev. Anthony B. Taylor, bishop of Little Rock
Pastoral Letter, *Welcome the Strangers Among Us*

to citizens and must not suspend them without legitimate reasons (CCC, 2237). Citizens, on the other hand, are obliged under the fourth commandment to respect lawful authority and to serve the common good by such means as paying taxes, voting, and defending their country (CCC, 2239-2240). Citizens are, however, entitled and even obliged at times to criticize government when it does not act in the public interest, and they are not required to obey any law or directive that conflicts with the natural moral law, the fundamental rights of human beings, or the teachings of the gospel (CCC, 2238, 2242).

Inasmuch as the duties of families apply to the community at large and even to nations as a whole, "more prosperous nations are obliged, to the extent they are able, to welcome the *foreigner* in search of the security and the means of livelihood which he cannot find in his country of origin" (CCC, 2241). Governments have a right to put in place reasonable regulations regarding immigration, and immigrants have the same obligations as native people do to respect the laws and accept the responsibilities of living in their adopted homelands. Moreover, we all share in the obligation of hospitality toward immigrants and are forbidden to economically or politically exploit them or to discriminate against them on the basis of their ethnicity, nationality, language, or religion. We are called not only to refrain from harassing immigrants but to welcome them in our churches and our communities and assist them in navigating life in an unfamiliar place. "The 'foreigner' is God's messenger who surprises us and interrupts the regularity and logic of daily life, bringing near those who are far away. In 'foreigners' the Church sees Christ who 'pitches His tent among us' and who 'knocks at our door' " (*Erga migrantes caritas Christi*, 99, 101).

Sharing Questions

- When have you struggled with issues of authority either inside or outside of your family? When haven't you?

- If your parents were immigrants, where did they come from, and what was their experience in their new country?

- How has your parish reached out to people from other countries who have moved into your community? What part have you played, or would you like to play, in this ministry?

Living the Good News

Jesus emphasized the connection between faith and action, between what we believe and what we do. In that spirit, decide on an individual or group action that flows from what you have shared in this session. If you decide to act on your own, share your decision with the group. If you decide on a group action, determine among you whether individual members will take responsibility for various aspects of the action.

You are likely to benefit most from taking an action that arises from your own response to the session. However, you can consider one of the following suggestions or use these ideas to help develop one of your own:

- Contact a family member with whom you have lost touch or whom you haven't spoken to because of a disagreement.

- Spend a quiet evening with your family, sharing what it means to be family to one another; if you are not with your family, choose to spend a quiet evening with a close friend.

- Select one action you could do to help a family in one of its struggles. For example, offer to take a young child for a day for a parent who is under stress.

- The challenges of welcoming new people into a community are vividly portrayed in the documentary film *Scenes from a Parish*, which follows the experiences of parishioners of St. Patrick's Church in the former mill town of Lawrence, Mass. The film examines the challenge of the commandment to love your neighbor when the ethnicity and the social and economic standing of your neighbors are changing – and your city and parish are changing as a result. Introduce your parish to RENEW International's Faith-Sharing Edition DVD of *Scenes from a Parish*, accompanied by a guide to building faith-sharing sessions using the film. Details on page 115.

- Visit a nursing home and make a lonely elderly person a part of your family.

In light of this session, this week I commit to:

_____

_____

Lifting Our Hearts

Offer spontaneous petitions or prayers of gratitude for specific members of your family, naming the ways in which they have blessed your life.

The leader designates one participant to begin the following prayer. Take turns reading the sections.

Voice 1	Ever-present God, you watch over us tenderly. Teach us what it means to have a compassionate heart.
Voice 2	The most expressed virtues of Jesus, your Son, who came to teach us about you were compassion and forgiveness.
Voice 3	How often we forget these virtues in dealing with those we love the most.
Voice 4	Help us to be compassionate and forgiving with the members of our own families.
Voice 5	Grant us the grace to be patient with the elderly, loving toward the little ones, and understanding with teenagers.
Voice 6	Help us to see the virtue of being gentle with ourselves so we can be gentle with others. We ask this through Jesus Christ, our Lord.
All	**Amen.**

Looking Ahead

- Prepare for your next session by prayerfully reading and studying:
    - Session 9: Chastity and Marital Fidelity
    - John 15: 9-17 ("Love one another as I have loved you")
    - *The Collegeville Bible Commentary: New Testament* by Robert J. Karris, for insight into the passage from the Gospel of John.
    - *United States Catholic Catechism for Adults*, summary of doctrinal statements, pp. 414-415 on the sixth commandment and pp. 444-445 on the ninth commandment.

- You may want to consult the relevant chapters in the *United States Catholic Catechism for Adults*: Chapter 30 "The Sixth Commandment: Marital Fidelity" and Chapter 33 "The Ninth Commandment: Practice Purity of Heart."

- You may also like to consult the relevant paragraphs from the *Catechism of the Catholic Church*, paragraphs 2331-2400 on the sixth commandment and paragraphs 2514-2533 on the ninth commandment.

- Remember to use RENEWING FAMILY FAITH and its helpful suggestions on how to extend the fruits of your sharing beyond your group, especially to your families (see page 114).

Chastity and Marital Fidelity

The sixth and ninth commandments

Suggested Environment

You may have a Bible and a candle on a small table, with the Bible opened to the Scripture text for this session. Consider decorating the table with the color of the liturgical season. You may display two wedding rings on a pillow. You may also provide three candles, light two, and invite two members of the group, a symbol of marital unity, to use the two lit candles to ignite the third.

It is helpful to have available the Catechism of the Catholic Church (CCC) *and the* United States Catholic Catechism for Adults (USCCA).

Lifting Our Hearts

Song Suggestion

"Blest Are Those Who Love You," Marty Haugen

Prayer

Pray together

Loving God,
we ask for your grace and strength
to live lives of chastity and love.
Help us to hold others and ourselves in reverence.
Instill in us a desire
to respond to your grace
and to be selfless and integrated
in our love for others. Amen.

Sharing Our Good News

Share how you did with your Living the Good News *from the previous session.*

Reflection 1

"Ordinary lives," extraordinary results

Louis Martin and Celia Guérin had something in common: both of them wanted to enter religious life, and neither was admitted. The chastity of monastic vows was not for them, but the chastity of marriage vows was. The rest of their story is that they met, fell in love, married, had children, worked, and lived lives of faithfulness to God and to each other. Louis was born in Bordeaux in 1823, and Celia, also called Azélie, was born in Gandelain, Normandy, in 1831. When Louis was 22, he sought to enter a religious order but was refused because he did not know Latin. He studied the language unsuccessfully for a year and worked thereafter as a watchmaker and jeweler. Celia, whose family had chronic financial difficulties, contributed to its support by learning Alençon point–a famous type of lace-making. Louis and Celia met in 1858 and were married. They continued working at their crafts, and they also maintained a full spiritual life– attending daily Mass, participating in personal and communal prayer, frequently receiving the Sacrament of Penance, and taking part in the activities of their parish. They had nine children, four of whom died prematurely. The other five, Louise, Pauline, Léonie, Céline, and Thérèse, all became nuns. The youngest is known to us as St. Thérèse of Lisieux, spiritual writer and Doctor of the Church. Celia died in 1877, and Louis raised the children in Lisieux with the help of Celia's brother and sister-in-law. Louis died in 1894. By wholeheartedly embracing the sacred nature of their marriage, Louis and Celia grew in holiness and nurtured the spirituality of their children. Through seemingly ordinary lives, they contributed enormously to their parish, their community, and to the world at large. Luis Martin and Celia Guérin were beatified in 2008 by Cardinal Jose Saraiva Martins, one of only two married couples to be so honored.

Sharing Question

- What can a 21st century couple learn from Louis Martin and Celia Guérin about fully integrating religious faith into everyday life?

"You shall not commit adultery." (Exodus 20:14)
"You shall not covet your neighbor's wife." (Exodus 20:17)

As followers of Jesus, we believe that love is the foundation of all the commandments. This is certainly clear in the sixth and ninth commandments with their implications for human relationships and sexuality. These commandments address the expression of love, solidarity, and fidelity between women and men that we see in the model of Louis Martin and Celia Guérin. Our physical being–including our sexuality–is made by God and is therefore good in itself, no matter how the idea of sexuality might be distorted by some elements of society. "Hence, we do not approach sexuality with fear or with hostility to the flesh. It is a gift of God by which men and women participate in his saving plan and respond to his call to grow in holiness" (*USCCA*, p. 405). Still, sexuality involves the whole person, body and soul. It concerns our emotional lives, our capacity to love and to parent children, and our ability to form bonds with other people (*CCC*, 2332).

In these commandments, God calls all Christians to lives of chastity. While this means that unmarried persons including single people, women and men who have taken religious vows, and homosexual persons should refrain from sexual activity, the term has an even broader and deeper meaning for all Christians. Chastity means integrating sexuality within our whole human nature, our whole person. "The acquisition of chastity depends on self-discipline and leads

Spotlight on the *Catechism*

"The many ways in which one can depart from God's call to chastity and marital fidelity are more than evident in American culture. The exploitation of sexuality for commercial gain is manifested in countless ads and other means of engaging our attention through television and allied media. The cult of the body, not just for health reasons but for hedonistic attraction, is a prime example of the effect of an exaggerated focus on sex and sexuality.

What is needed is a healing vision of sexuality, the body and the human person. Pope John Paul II offers us this perspective in his theology of the body. He begins with the idea that God willed each human being for his or her own sake. This means that none of us is merely a part of something else, or a means of gaining some result. God created us as free and unique human persons. We are not things to be used, but persons to be respected."

United States Catholic Catechism for Adults, p. 412

to an internal freedom, which enables human beings to temper sexual desires according to God's plan for the appropriate expression of love in the marital relationship of a man and a woman" (*USCCA*, p. 405). What chastity means to any individual man or woman depends on the circumstances of that person's life–and these circumstances inevitably change over time. The *Catechism* points out, in fact, that a person does not acquire chastity once and for all at a particular point but sustains the effort through a lifetime (*CCC*, 2342). Living a chaste life means using sexuality only as an unselfish expression of love for another. Sins against chastity include incest, sexual abuse, pornography, masturbation, prostitution and rape. These are by nature selfish acts in which the needs, the dignity, and even the physical and emotional wellbeing of the other are often ignored or directly violated (*USCCA*, pp. 406-407; *CCC*, 2351-2356)

God has given us sexual energy that is designed to foster good, healthy, and life-giving relationships. Our sexual energy is not limited to sexual intercourse. We also express it in a broad range of human activity. Meaningful work in the service of others is a healthy way to express the sexual energy God has given us. Building the human family involves the development of personal and committed relationships with the poor and the needy. This is characterized by dedicated service and sacrificial love.

Sexuality is also an important aspect of our relationship with God. The process of accepting our sexuality helps us to be in touch with our true selves, enabling us to be dynamic and honest in our communication with God and in other close relationships. Accepting the fact that we are sexual beings helps us to gain a humble awareness of our own weakness, neediness, and dependence on the patient mercy of God. Our experience of trying to live a chaste life teaches us to be patient, forgiving, and loving with one another, as God is patient, forgiving, and loving with us.

To the extent that we free ourselves of the destructive urges of our human nature and use God's gifts unselfishly, we can achieve what Jesus wanted for us: "I came that they may have life, and have it abundantly" (*Jn* 10:10).

Sharing Question

- According to the *Catechism of the Catholic Church*, we grow in chastity throughout our lives. How is that lived in the 21st century?

Pondering the Word

"Abide in my love"

As Christians, we are called to face the difficulties of prayer with humility, with trust in God, and with perseverance. One step toward improving our prayer life is examining our priorities, as Jesus explains so clearly in this gospel passage:

John 15:9-17

Sharing Questions

• Take a moment to reflect on what word, phrase, or image from the Scripture passage touches your heart or speaks to your life. Reflect on this in silence, or share it aloud.

• In the gospel passage we just read, Jesus challenges us to love one another as God loves us. What are some of the things that help us form healthy relationships with others?

Reflection 2

Sex and love a single gift

Through married love, a woman and a man give themselves totally to each other. They become one flesh (*Gn* 2:24) and Jesus has taught us that their bond can be broken only by death (*Mk* 10:9), and that bond matures and deepens with time and experience. "Acceptance of a spouse's faults and failures as well as one's own is a recognition that the call to holiness in marriage is a lifelong process of conversion and growth" (*USCCA*, p. 408). This covenant between wife and husband has two purposes. One is the love and faithfulness that the couple shares, fully involving their "minds, hearts, emotions, bodies, souls and aspirations" (*USCCA*, p. 408). The other is the conception, birth, and education of children. These two aspects of the marriage bond are inseparable. For that reason, artificial contraception and methods, such as *in vitro* fertilization, of conceiving a child without intercourse are contrary to Church teaching, because they break the link between conception and sexual union. God calls the couple to be always open to the children he may give them, not as a right but as a gift. "In giving birth to children and educating and forming them, they cooperate with the love of God" and become an image of the creative power and life of the Holy Trinity (*USCCA*, p. 409).

Spouses give each other the gifts of self and life

"In its most profound reality, love is essentially a gift; and conjugal love, while leading the spouses to the reciprocal 'knowledge' which makes them 'one flesh,' does not end with the couple, because it makes them capable of the greatest possible gift, the gift by which they become cooperators with God for giving life to a new human person. Thus the couple, while giving themselves to one another, give not just themselves but also the reality of children, who are a living reflection of their love, a permanent sign of conjugal unity and a living and inseparable synthesis of their being a father and a mother.

When they become parents, spouses receive from God the gift of a new responsibility. Their parental love is called to become for the children the visible sign of the very love of God, 'from whom every family in heaven and on earth is named.'

It must not be forgotten however that, even when procreation is not possible, conjugal life does not for this reason lose its value. Physical sterility in fact can be for spouses the occasion for other important services to the life of the human person, for example, adoption, various forms of educational work, and assistance to other families and to poor or handicapped children."

Familiaris Consortio, Pope John Paul II, 14

In a committed relationship, the sexual act is sacramental and brings the married couple to the depths of love and gratitude and opens them to be a blessing to each other and to the world. Ideally, it makes them more generous, patient, and loving with each other, with their children, and with others. When sexual intercourse, even in marriage, is practiced without a sense of personal responsibility or loving commitment, it becomes merely the occasion for personal pleasure achieved with the help of a partner. When the pursuit of one partner's personal pleasure becomes the primary focus of sexual expression, the entire structure of the marriage is seriously weakened. It is no longer the earthly sign of the loving self-sacrifice in the relationship between Christ and his bride, the Church.

The image of Christ and his Church is a model not only for the unselfish relationship in a marriage but also for the sanctity of the marriage bond itself. Taking that bond lightly is opposed to Christian values, because the marriage covenant between baptized Christians is the sacramental witness to Christ's faithfulness to his church (*CCC,* 2365).

Living a sexually moral life is a challenge for every person, regardless of religion, culture, marital status, or age. It is difficult today to develop good moral standards concerning sexuality because sexual mores are frequently debased and the sexual act is so casually separated from love. The idea that sex and love are separate experiences is propagated every day in newspapers and magazines, on television, in the movies, in popular music, and on the increasingly pervasive Internet. Regardless of popular culture, however, living a life of Christian chastity is a grace-filled response to the call of God. The teaching of the Church as well as the support of family members, good friends, or a small Christian community can be very helpful in this regard. They help us counteract the influences in our culture that do not value, or that even ridicule, this wonderful gift.

The *Catechism* instructs us on the importance of living an upright life rather than a double life (*CCC*, 2338). Sins such as adultery, promiscuity, fornication, prostitution, and rape are obviously opposed to the demands of love (*CCC*, 2353-2356). Pornography, too, which has become almost universally available through the expansion of the Internet and services such as "on-demand" movies, can lead a person into a "secret" life that involves solitary and therefore disordered sexual behavior such as masturbation. In the case of a married person, seeking out pornography deprives the spouse of the full commitment and affection that are essential to marriage. Pornography is a grave wrong also because it implies the sexual exploitation not only of adults, but often of children, and often leads to direct, criminal sexual exploitation either through on-line conversations–often accompanied by still photographs or video images–or through personal meetings.

The Church's teaching on issues such as extramarital and premarital sex are particularly at odds with the world's values and often cause tension for those sincerely trying to practice their faith. Couples who are engaged to be married, for example, should resist the practice of "living together" or "cohabitation" and uphold the sanctity of the union they are about to share, reserving for marriage the expressions of affection that belong only in married life (*CCC*, 2350). "Cohabitation does not guarantee successful married life, as has been revealed in the painful experience of many, and is detrimental to future commitment" (*USCCA*, pp. 410-411). For those already married, adultery is a flaunting of the faithfulness that is at the heart of the marriage vow. It is an act of injustice against the spouse, and it "weakens the institution of marriage and the stability of the family" (*USCCA*, p. 410). Often, it also involves exploitation of a third party.

As for divorce, the Church upholds the explicit teaching of Jesus that marriage is rooted in the natural law and is a union that cannot be dissolved, even in cases of adultery or abuse in which separation may be the most prudent course (cf. *Luke* 16:18). Marriage, in the Catholic tradition, reflects the covenant relationship between God and his people–a relationship that implies an exchange of total and unconditional love. When two baptized people are married according to the laws of the Catholic Church, the marriage is presumed to be valid–and therefore indissoluble–unless it is proven otherwise to a Church tribunal. A tribunal would declare a marriage null–in other words, declare that no marriage had occurred–if some impediment were proven. "Grounds for a declaration of nullity . . . include flaws in the rite itself, in the legal capacity of the parties to marry . . . or in the consent they gave–whether they were lacking in discretion or maturity of judgment or were marrying due to force or fear or with an intent to exclude fidelity or the commitment to a life long union or were placing unacceptable conditions on the marriage" (cf. *CCC*, 1628-1629) (*USCCA*, pp. 288-289).

The Church encourages us to have a positive attitude toward the human body while not losing our awareness that the body is susceptible to manipulation, exploitation, abuse, and control. It is important to get beyond the negative prescriptions–the things we are told we should not do–and come to a full appreciation of the positive and life-giving aspects of the Church's teaching (*CCC*, 2366-2372). The teaching on these two commandments, addressing the intimate love we have for each other and for God, shows clearly that the positive teachings of the Catholic faith can be both attractive and deeply meaningful.

Sharing Questions

• Whom do you know personally that exemplifies the virtue of chastity?

• What is it about Catholic teaching on sexuality that fosters a healthy generosity and unselfishness?

• How is the relationship between Christ and his Church a model for unselfish love?

Living the Good News

Jesus emphasized the connection between faith and action, between what we believe and what we do. In that spirit, decide on an individual or group action that flows from what you have shared in this session. If you decide to act on your own, share your decision with the group. If you decide on a group action, determine among you whether individual members will take responsibility for various aspects of the action.

You are likely to benefit most from taking an action that arises from your own response to the session. However, you can consider one of the following suggestions or use these ideas to help develop one of your own:

- If you are married, arrange to attend a Marriage Encounter weekend, a retreat, a workshop, or some other gathering to support your spiritual growth as a married couple.

- If you are single, arrange to attend a retreat or a gathering with others who are single to support your spiritual journey.

- If you are engaged, arrange to attend an Engaged Encounter weekend or a Pre-Cana Conference to prepare for your marriage. Ask your parish priest or a member of the parish staff for information.

- Take steps to speak out against pornography or immoral sexuality on television or on the Internet.

- Confront and boycott stores that sell pornographic material.

- Monitor your children's Internet activities and television viewing.

- Take time this week to support a married couple or a single person through a telephone call, letter, or e-mail.

- In your journaling, pay close attention to the joys and difficulties of your sexuality. Bring these insights to your prayer this week, giving thanks to God for this gift.

In light of this session, this week I commit to:

_____

_____

Lifting Our Hearts

Offer spontaneous prayer. Conclude with the Lord's Prayer.

End the session by affirming one another. Take time to say one affirming thing about each person in the group. Then give each other a sign of peace.

Looking Ahead

- Prepare for your next session by prayerfully reading and studying:

  - **Session 10: Creating a Culture of Life**

  - Matthew 5:21-24, 38-42, and 43-48 (Jesus' teaching about anger, retaliation, and love of enemies)

  - *The Collegeville Bible Commentary: New Testament* by Robert J. Karris, for insight into the passage from the Gospel of Matthew.

  - *United States Catholic Catechism for Adults*, summary of doctrinal statements for the fifth commandment, pp. 400-401, and for the eighth commandment, pp. 436-437.

- You may also like to consult the relevant chapters from the *United States Catholic Catechism for Adults*: Chapter 29 "The Fifth Commandment: Promote the Culture of Life," and Chapter 32 "The Eighth Commandment: Tell the Truth."

- You may also like to consult the relevant paragraphs from the *Catechism of the Catholic Church*, paragraphs 2258-2330 on the fifth commandment and paragraphs 2464-2513 on the eighth commandment.

- Remember to use Renewing Family Faith and its helpful suggestions on how to extend the fruits of your sharing beyond your group, especially to your families (see page 114).

SESSION TEN

Creating a Culture of Life

The fifth and eighth commandments

Suggested Environment

You may have a Bible and a candle on a small table, with the Bible opened to the Scripture text for this session. Consider decorating the table with the color of the liturgical season. You may also set out stones with words inscribed on them denoting death in some way–for example, war, euthanasia, abortion, capital punishment, loneliness, or illness.

It is helpful to have available the Catechism of the Catholic Church (CCC) *and the* United States Catholic Catechism for Adults (USCCA).

Lifting Our Hearts

Song Suggestion

"Prayer of St. Francis," Sebastian Temple

Prayer

Pray together

Almighty God,
as we come together to reflect on your commandments,
we praise you and thank you for the gift of life.

We hear you call us to protect life –
life still unborn, life condemned,
life threatened by age and illness,

81

life diminished by poverty and oppression,
life menaced by violence and by war.

You who have given us life,
give us the courage to defend life
in all of its stages.

We ask this through our Lord Jesus Christ,
who is the way, and the truth, and the life.
Amen.

Sharing Our Good News

Share how you did with your Living the Good News *from the previous session.*

Reflection 1

A challenging model

Maria Teresa Goretti was one of the youngest persons ever canonized by the Catholic Church. Maria was born in 1890 in the Province of Le Marche in Italy, but when she was 12 years old, she was living with her impoverished family near the coast of the Tyrrhenian Sea. Her father had died of malaria in 1900, and she was caring for her younger sister when a young man, Alessandro Serenelli, whose family shared quarters with the Gorettis, forced Maria into the house and tried to sexually assault her. When she resisted, he stabbed her numerous times, and she died the next day. Before she died, she forgave Serenelli, who was subsequently sentenced to thirty years in prison. Serenelli, who reported meeting Maria in a dream, expressed remorse for his crimes. He asked the Goretti family to forgive him, and Maria's mother, Assunta, explicitly did so. When Serenelli had been released, he provided testimony for the beatification of Maria. He later went to live at a Capuchin community and spent the rest of his life working there as a gardener and receptionist. Maria Goretti was canonized in 1950 by Pope Pius XII. On the 100th anniversary of her death, Pope John Paul II took note of the mercy shown by Maria and her mother in the face of such brutality. "The divine indulgence for human shortcomings is a demanding model of behavior for all believers," the pope said, and added: "May humanity start out with determination on the way of mercy and forgiveness."

Sharing Question

• Maria and Assunta Goretti forgave Alessandro Serenelli for serious and irreversible crimes. Recall and share a time when you were able to forgive a serious wrong committed against you, against someone you know, or even against a stranger or a whole community.

"You shall not murder. . . ." (Exodus 20:13)

Human life is sacred, because it is created by God in his own likeness. Therefore, everyone must respect the dignity of human life, and no one has the right to willfully destroy an innocent human being (*CCC*, 2258). Only in limited circumstances may we take action that results in death that we do not directly intend. One example is self-defense against an unjust aggressor (*CCC*, 2263-2265). Another example is execution of a prisoner, although the Church teaches that this remedy should be used only if the death penalty is the only way to protect the public from a dangerous criminal (*CCC*, 2266-2267). Even at that, the Church argues that non-lethal means of punishment are preferable (*CCC*, 2267).

Social values are not always in harmony with these gospel values, and the fifth commandment calls us as Christians "to create the culture of life and work against the culture of death" (*USCCA*, p. 389). This refers to the struggle to uphold the sacredness of life from the moment of conception to the moment of death against the argument that there are "legitimate" reasons for directly killing innocent human beings: abortion, euthanasia, assisted suicide.

> "The protection of life is a seamless garment. You can't protect some life and not others."
>
> Eileen Egan, Catholic journalist (1912-2000)

The Church's position on abortion has been clear from the beginning. The *Didache*, a catechism written around the end of the first century, is explicit: "You shall not kill the embryo by abortion" (*Didache* 2,2: SCh 248, 148; cf. *Ep. Barnabae* 19, 5: PG 2, 777; *Ad Diognetum* 5, 6: PG 2, 1173; Tertullian, *Apol.* 9: PL 1, 319-320.) (*CCC*, 2271). From the first moment of existence, "a human being must be recognized as having the rights of a person–among which is the inviolable right of every innocent being to life" (Cf. CDF, *Donum vita* I, 1.) (*CCC*, 2270), and respecting this right means neither undergoing nor cooperating in an abortion (*CCC*, 2272).

While science brings us benefits, it also conflicts at times with the moral law–for example, with respect to *in vitro* fertilization,

Adults must protect children from 'bloodless violence'

"Bullying has been a part of young lives for as long as we can remember. Now, with the Web, it has a huge impact. Someone making fun of you to a few people when you're a teen is troublesome; having someone bad mouth you to half the world via Twitter and Facebook is overwhelming. The huge impact of such bloodless violence calls for stepped up protections, perhaps safeguards or monitoring for the Web. Parents and educators need to assert themselves in this regard. Just as they wouldn't permit children to beat one another to a pulp on the front lawn, they have to be sure their children aren't pummeling one another in cyberspace."

Sister Mary Ann Walsh, RSM
Director of Media Relations, USCCB

stem-cell research, and cloning. *In vitro* fertilization, a method of achieving conception outside of sexual intercourse, often results in the destruction of eggs that have been fertilized and are beginning to grow as human persons. "This action is the taking of human life and is gravely sinful" (*USCCA*, p. 392). Stem-cell research shows promise of treatments for diseases such as Parkinson's and Alzheimer's. Stem cells are found in several parts of the human body, but the insistence of some scientists that cells are best obtained from human embryos conflicts with the fifth commandment because an embryo has to be destroyed in order to obtain the cells. "But every embryo from the moment of conception has the entire genetic makeup of a unique human life. The growing child must be recognized and treated as completely human" (*USCCA*, p. 392).

Other practices that disregard the sanctity of life are euthanasia or "mercy killing" and physician-assisted suicide. "Regardless of the motives or means, euthanasia consists of putting to death those who are sick, are disabled, or are dying. It is morally unacceptable" (*USCCA*, p. 393). Physician-assisted suicide is also prohibited by the fifth commandment. The *Catechism* explains that all human beings are responsible for protecting the lives God gave us and that suicide under any circumstances is contrary to God's law (*CCC*, 2280-2281). Still, the Church recognizes the psychological and physical strains that might drive people to suicide. "By ways known to him alone, God can provide the opportunity for salutary repentance. The Church prays for persons who have taken their own lives" (*CCC*, 2283).

With respect to our stewardship over our own lives, as Catholic men and women we protect our health by eating and drinking moderately; by avoiding abuse of tobacco, alcohol, or drugs, or by refraining from driving recklessly or acting in any other way that puts our safety or that of others in danger (*CCC*, 2290). As members of a society and as individuals, we Catholics also do what we can to help others attain the "food and clothing, housing, health care, basic education, employment, and social assistance" they need to lead healthy and productive lives (*CCC*, 2288).

We accept medical procedures that may heal us or those whose care is our responsibility. However, we may reject procedures that serve only to prolong the dying process. The decision concerning such treatment is left up to patients, if they are able to state their wishes or have prepared an advance medical directive, or to those legally entitled to act on their behalf (*CCC*, 2276-2279). Ordinary treatment–food, water, warmth, and hygiene–is morally required for the dying. However, extraordinary treatment may not be required and can even be discontinued, depending on how treatment is likely to help the patient or what kind of burden it might impose on the patient and the patient's family. "For example, in instances when a person has been declared brain-dead, the patient can be disconnected from mechanical devices that sustain breathing and the heart since there is little hope of the person's recovery" (*USCCA*, p. 394).

The fifth commandment also expresses God's will with respect to preserving peace and avoiding war. "The best way to avoid war is . . . by letting go of the anger and hatred that breed war and by eliminating the poverty, injustice, and deprivation of human rights that lead to war" (*USCCA*, p. 395). The Church has long taught that certain conditions may justify "legitimate defense by military force" (*CCC*, 2309), but there is a grave danger in modern warfare because it enables those who possess scientific weapons to commit serious crimes against innocent people (*CCC*, 2307-2317). And even in the absence of war itself, "the arms race is an utterly treacherous trap for humanity, and one which ensnares the poor to an intolerable degree" (*Gaudium et spes* 81 § 3).

One of the most challenging passages in the gospels is Jesus' commentary on the fifth commandment. The commandment is brief, blunt, and–to most human beings–obvious. Murder, the malicious and premeditated taking of an innocent life, is almost universally rejected by individuals and by nations. In the Sermon on the Mount, however, Jesus expanded the spirit of the commandment far beyond its literal meaning. Not only are we not to commit physical violence against each other, he said, we are not even to speak or think "violently" about each other, whether that takes the form of anger, hatred, envy, or resentment (*CCC*, 2258-2262). This commandment also means that we must not subject each other to–or tolerate–psychological violence such as bullying whether in person or via the Internet.

Spotlight on the *Catechism*

"The pro-life commitment of the Church is reflected in her compassion for those who so often regret having had an abortion, her understanding for those who are facing difficult decisions, and her assistance for all who choose life. People who have been involved with an abortion are encouraged to get in touch the Project Rachel ministry and other ministries that enable them to seek the mercy of God in the Sacrament of Penance and Reconciliation and to obtain the necessary counseling. Pro-life ministries work with expectant mothers who are considering abortion by encouraging them to choose life for their children. They also provide alternatives to abortion through prenatal care, assistance in raising children, and adoption placement services."

United States Catholic Catechism for Adults, pp. 391-392

In light of this commandment, the Catechism explains that there is a difference between anger and justice. When one person has harmed another, a penalty or some sort of restitution might be appropriate, but revenge–including violence–as a way to satisfy anger is morally wrong (*CCC*, 2302). In the same way, deliberate hatred of another person, for any reason, to the point of wishing that person harm is a serious sin (*CCC*, 2303).

Sharing Question

• Creating a culture of life is very challenging. What are some of your questions or struggles with this issue?

Pondering the Word

"Go also the second mile"
Matthew 5:21-24, 38-42, and 43-48

Sharing Questions

• Take a moment to reflect on what word, phrase, or image from the Scripture passage touches your heart or speaks to your life. Reflect on this in silence, or share it aloud.

• Recall and share a time when you struggled with anger, resentment, hatred, or vengeance.

Reflection 2

"So help me God"

"You shall not bear false witness against your neighbor." (Exodus 20:16)

The eighth commandment presents us with a clear standard to live by: Always tell the truth; never lie. That's a basic requirement of human relationships. The purpose of speech–and, by extension, the purpose of writing and all other forms of human communication–is for us to share with each other what we know to be true. Unfortunately, the means of communication are often used to obscure the truth or to disseminate information that is simply false. When that happens and we recognize it, our trust in the source of false information is eroded or destroyed (*CCC*, 2464-2469).

Anyone who deliberately leads another person into error by saying things that are not true, or by withholding important information that is true, violates this commandment (*CCC*, 2485). People also sin against the truth when they ruin the reputation of another by telling lies, when they believe negative things about another without a sufficient basis, when they unjustly reveal another person's faults, or when they lie under oath, orally or in writing (*USCCA*, p. 432). In addition to telling the truth when we speak, the eighth commandment requires us to keep secrets justly entrusted to us–including professional secrets–and to respect the privacy of others by keeping to ourselves anything that might unnecessarily embarrass them or otherwise harm them (*CCC*, 2488-2489, 2491-2492).

The eighth commandment applies to mass communications just as it applies to personal and professional communications. Those who disseminate information or express their viewpoints in print media, on television, on the Internet, or through any of the electronic devices that have become a part of everyday life are bound to tell the truth and to avoid presenting as truth what is actually interpretation, speculation, or opinion. "Though the intuition remains that there is really such a thing as objective truth, it tends to be lost in a marathon of inconclusive discussions. . . . Much of what passes for truth is the effort to justify individual behavior. In its unsettling form, this generates an attitude of skepticism and even suspicion about any truth claims. Thus objective truth is considered unattainable" (*USCCA*, pp. 435-436). For example, some will justify abortion by arguing that the beginning of human life at conception is a matter of opinion.

As advances in technology make the exchange of facts and ideas both easier and more far-reaching, the need to recognize the responsibility that goes along with that activity becomes more urgent (*CCC*, 2493-2494). This is true of private citizens, professional communicators, and public officials. Because the words and images that circulate so freely and in such volume in our time frequently have content that is not in tune with the gospel, we need to be careful about what we read, listen to, and watch. The Internet, in particular, has become a conduit for opinion presented as though it were fact and a means for anonymous writers to slander people who have no recourse. Most important, we need to reflect seriously before we draw conclusions so that we do not form our consciences based on false or unwholesome influences (*CCC*, 2496).

Sharing Questions

- We are called as Christians to witness to the truth of the gospel of Jesus. Through this witness, we transmit our faith by what we say and what we do. Recall a time when you witnessed to your faith in words or actions.

- How is telling the truth a matter of justice?

- What can you do to challenge the media to greater honesty and integrity?

Living the Good News

Jesus emphasized the connection between faith and action, between what we believe and what we do. In that spirit, decide on an individual or group action that flows from what you have shared in this session. If you decide to act on your own, share your decision with the group. If you decide on a group action, determine among you whether individual members will take responsibility for various aspects of the action.

You are likely to benefit most from taking an action that arises from your own response to the session. However, you can consider one of the following suggestions or use these ideas to help develop one of your own:

- Contact the Secretariat for Pro-Life Activities for information on supporting life issues. Decide how you can support a culture of life. (Secretariat for Pro-Life Activities, U.S. Conference of Catholic Bishops, 3211 Fourth Street, N.E., Washington, D.C. 20017-1194. Phone: 202-541-3070. Fax: 202-541-3054. Web site: www.uccb.org/prolife

- Learn about advanced directives for health care. Let your doctors and relatives know your wishes.

- Offer assistance to a pregnant woman who is struggling to have her baby, or to a group home that supports pregnant women.

- Write to television stations and supporting sponsors when you find programs or commercials offensive because of violence, explicit sexuality, or other content that is inconsistent with the gospel.

- Use and promote newspapers, magazines, and other media that have integrity.

In light of this session, this week I commit to:

_____

_____

Lifting Our Hearts

Take turns praying the following intercessions for life. All respond, **"Lord, hear our prayer."**

For all children who have died from abortion,
that God may cradle them in his arms
and grant them eternal peace with him,
we pray to the Lord. . . **R**

For all mothers,
especially those who are young or alone,
beaten or addicted;
that God might heal their broken hearts
and seal them with his love;
we pray to the Lord. . . **R**

For fathers,
especially those who are very young,
that through the intercession of St. Joseph
they might assume the great responsibility

which God has given to them,
we pray to the Lord. . . *R*

For the bishops and priests of our Church,
that by their commitment to the innocent child
the Gospel of Life might be preached
in each of our churches,
we pray to the Lord. . . *R*

For the justices of our Supreme Court,
and the members of our Congress,
that the silent voice of the unborn child
might move their hearts and minds,
we pray to the Lord. . . *R*

For the children of our country,
especially those who are forgotten or neglected,
that their presence might remind us
of the infinite value of human life,
we pray to the Lord. . . *R*

For the men and women on death row
awaiting the end of their lives,
that we might pray for them
with compassion and care;
we pray to the Lord. . . *R*

For those deprived of their human needs
and their human rights,
that they may be given the dignity
which God confers on all his people;
we pray to the Lord. . . *R*

For all who are forgotten or thrown away,
and especially for the poor, the sick and the aged,
that God might change our hearts
and move us to love them as the image of Christ
We pray to the Lord. . . *R*

For doctors, nurses and other medical personnel,
especially those tempted by abortion,
that God might change their hearts
and give them the conviction of the Gospel of Life,
we pray to the Lord. . . *R*

Adapted from Respect Life 2000 Liturgy Guide
Secretariat for Pro-Life Activities, USCCB, Washington, DC

*To conclude, pray the Lord's Prayer and offer each other a
sign of God's peace.*

Looking Ahead

- Prepare for your next session by prayerfully reading and studying:

    - **Session 11: Stewards of God's Gifts**

    - Luke 19:1-10 (the encounter between Jesus and Zaccheus)

    - the summary of doctrinal statements on the
      seventh commandment, *United States Catholic Catechism
      for Adults*, p. 426.

- You may like to consult the *United States Catholic Catechism
  for Adults*, Chapter 31, "The Seventh Commandment: Do Not Steal–
  Act Justly."

- You may also like to consult the *Catechism of the Catholic Church*,
  paragraphs 2401-2463 on the seventh commandment.

- Remember to use RENEWING FAMILY FAITH and its helpful suggestions
  on how to extend the fruits of your sharing beyond your group,
  especially to your families (see page 114).

Stewards of God's Gifts

The seventh commandment

Suggested Environment

You may have a Bible and a candle on a small table, with the Bible opened to the Scripture text for this session. Consider decorating the table with the color of the liturgical season. You may also display symbols of work, such as kitchen utensils, a spade, a hammer, a file folder, or a teacher's manual.

It is helpful to have available the Catechism of the Catholic Church (CCC) *and the* United States Catholic Catechism for Adults (USCCA).

Lifting Our Hearts

Song Suggestion

"Lord, You Have Come," Cesário Gabaráin

Prayer

Pray together

O Father, Creator of all,
we ask you as we gather here
to transform us into the image of your Son.
May we put on the mind of Christ.
May our hands be those of Christ.

Dear God, give us the conviction
that the world was created as a gift from you to all.
To live in peace, joy, and harmony
means it is essential that all the goods of the earth be shared.

Help us, O Holy Spirit,
to change our selfish attitudes.

Sometimes we want to blame the victims,
those who are suffering.
Teach us compassion for all hurting people.

Give us the heart of Christ.
Teach us to use the world's goods respectfully.
Help us to share.
We ask this in Jesus' name. Amen

Sharing Our Good News

Share how you did with your Living the Good News *from the previous session.*

Reflection 1

The world belongs to all

The most unlikely figure in the National Cowgirl Hall of Fame in Fort Worth, Texas, is probably a French Canadian woman in the traditional habit of a 19th century Roman Catholic nun. She was born Esther Pariseau in 1823 near Saint-Elzéar in southeastern Quebec, but she made her mark at the other end of the continent as Mother Joseph. Esther's dad, who was a carriage maker, taught her carpentry to go along with her other practical skills: reading, writing, calculating, sewing, cooking, spinning, and housekeeping. In 1843, she joined the Sisters of Providence in Montreal. Thirteen years later, she and three other sisters travelled across the continent to Vancouver, Washington, where they transformed an old building into a convent. Mother Joseph herself built the chapel and its altar. The sisters ministered to the sick, assisted Native Americans who had been driven off their land, cared for orphans, and educated boys and girls. Mother Joseph opened the first permanent school and the first permanent hospital in the Northwest and went on to build other hospitals, orphanages, schools, homes for the aged, and shelters for mentally ill people in an area encompassing Washington, Oregon, Idaho, and Montana. Mother Joseph was often the architect and construction supervisor on these projects. She personally raised money for this work by traveling through the mining camps in the region, braving bad weather, wolves, and robbers. Mother Joseph died in 1902. In 1980, the State of Washington donated a statue of her to be placed in Statuary Hall in the U.S. Senate. In 1981, she was inducted into the Cowgirl Hall of Fame for her "monumental contributions to health care, education, and social projects throughout the Northwest."

Sharing Question

• How does the work of Mother Joseph and her sisters in the harsh conditions of the 19th century Northwest affect your feeling about the challenges of poverty in our own time?

"You shall not steal." (Exodus 20:15)

The fundamental meaning of the seventh commandment is clear: God forbids us to unjustly take anything that belongs to another person. That includes not only outright stealing, but such behavior as deliberately keeping things that were borrowed, or keeping found things when one knows the owner or does not make a sincere effort to find the owner. "Theft includes not only robbery but also actions such as embezzlement, computer theft, counterfeit money, fraud, identity theft, copyright violations (including pirating such things as music or computer software), and mail scams" (*USCCA*, p. 419).

However, the commandment reaches even beyond these matters and directs us not to wrong our neighbors in any way with respect to what is rightly theirs—and what is rightly theirs may include property and funds. It can even include time when it comes to just compensation for labor (*CCC*, 2401, 2408-2409).

The commandment addresses many aspects of everyday life. For example, it forbids dishonesty in business, whether on the part of the buyer or the seller; the buyer should pay and the seller should charge fair prices for goods or services. This commandment forbids schemes in which people are enticed to invest their money in non-existent enterprises; it forbids attempts to lure people into taking on debt that they can't afford—such as the subprime mortgages that helped bring on the American housing crisis in the first decade of the century. The commandment forbids paying wages that deprive workers of fair compensation for their time and labor. It also forbids inflating prices to take undue advantage of shortages in supply or to exploit consumers whose options or mobility may be limited—a common condition among economically depressed populations (*CCC*, 2409).

The seventh commandment requires that both parties to contracts, including mortgages and other legally constituted loans, live up to their obligations (*CCC*, 2410-2411). The commandment requires us to take care of the property of others when it is in our possession–an apartment or a rented car, for example–and to make restitution to the owner for any property that we may have damaged or unjustly taken (CCC, 2411-2412), as Zacchaeus promised to do after Jesus called him down from the sycamore tree (*Lk* 19:8).

Sharing Question

• How can the practice of the seventh commandment contribute to peace and equality in our communities?

Pondering the Word

"I came to seek the lost"

A tax collector like Zacchaeus was disliked because he was considered a collaborator with the Roman occupiers and because he was suspected of adding to the tax so that he could keep the excess for himself. Zacchaeus climbed a tree to see what Jesus was like. In the process of meeting Jesus, he gained new insights. What insights can you gain from listening to this story?

Luke: 19:1-10

Sharing Questions

• Take a moment to reflect on what word, phrase, or image from the Scripture passage touches your heart or speaks to your life. Reflect on this in silence, or share it aloud.

• Zacchaeus looked back at his dealings and made up for any injustice he may have committed. In what ways can we be good stewards of what God has given us–wealth, property, time, talents?

Reflection 2

The earth: God's gift to everyone

The Church teaches that God did not create the world for only a few, but for everyone. The seventh commandment underlies that concept, requiring us to respect all created things (CCC, 2416). That means that we should conserve natural resources and protect the environment. Littering, wasting water and electricity, improperly disposing of toxic wastes–including many household items, carelessly discarding things such as paper that can be recycled–avoiding these things means protecting everyone's rights in the natural world. "In this regard," Pope Benedict XVI has written, "it is essential to 'sense' that the earth is our 'common home' and, in our stewardship and service to all, to choose the path of dialogue rather than the path of unilateral decisions" (*The Human Family, a Community of Peace*, January 1, 2008).

The gift of the earth to all humanity is also the foundation of the right to our private property, but we must share the goods of the earth for the common welfare (*CCC*, 2402-2405). By this, the church does not mean that Christians are obliged to share only from their excess wealth; she means that we should imitate the example Jesus pointed out: the woman who gave her last two coins to support the temple. "This poor widow has put in more than all those who are contributing to the treasury," Jesus told his disciples. "For all of them have contributed out of their abundance; but she out of her poverty has put in everything she had, all she had to live on" (*Mk* 12:43-44). Jesus dramatized this concept when he used an inadequate supply of bread and fish to feed a crowd (*Mk* 8:1-9). Those who had caught those fish and baked that bread could not have imagined that the fruit of their work would be put to such use. The fact that it was is a sign to us that we are called to share the work of our hands, to feed one another. Opportunities to do this are as close as the nearest food pantry or thrift shop.

Widening the circle of our "neighbors"

"Many Catholics, at the urging of Our brother bishops, have contributed unstintingly to the assistance of the needy and have gradually widened the circle of those they call neighbors.

But these efforts, as well as public and private allocations of gifts, loans and investments, are not enough. It is not just a question of fighting wretched conditions, though this is an urgent and necessary task. It involves building a human community where men can live truly human lives, free from discrimination on account of race, religion or nationality, free from servitude to other men or to natural forces which they cannot yet control satisfactorily. It involves building a human community where liberty is not an idle word, where the needy Lazarus can sit down with the rich man at the same banquet table."

Pope Paul VI, *Populorum progression*, 46-47

The *Catechism* tells us that by our labor we continue God's own creative action and give thanks to God for the vitality and the talents he has given us. The *Catechism* recalls that Jesus himself worked, just as he experienced all the realities of human life (*CCC*, 2427).

The *Catechism* also points out that workers are not to be treated as if they were only the means to someone else's profit (*CCC*, 2414, 2424). This refers to human slavery, which persists in the world, but it also refers to any form of exploitation of labor. Employers and workers should recognize their mutual stewardship and mutual dependence on material resources and the means of production. When conflicts arise between employers and employees, both parties should try to resolve their differences through negotiation that respects the rights and duties of everyone involved (*CCC*, 2430).

Those who operate businesses or industries, and those whom they employ, must not deprive the community of the benefits of the created world by polluting or otherwise damaging the environment. They are required to balance the legitimate need for profit with the rights and wellbeing of individual people and of society in general (*CCC*, 2432).

All people are entitled to have access to employment and to professions and must not be excluded because of discrimination based on gender, race, religion, nationality, or irrelevant physical condition (*CCC*, 2433). Once employed, a person is entitled under this commandment to a just wage, based on the worker's needs and contributions. Here, too, there must be no discrimination: women, for example, must not be paid less than men for doing the same or equivalent work; nor should women be denied promotions or other advancement on the basis of their gender. The *Catechism* notes that the fact that a worker agrees to a wage does not, in itself, make that wage just, an important consideration (*CCC*, 2434).

Poor people, including immigrants, who lack political and social leverage often accept jobs out of their need for any work at all; under this commandment, taking advantage of such people by paying them less than their labor is worth is a serious wrong.

The *Catechism* reminds us, too, that we are part of an international community. Many of the problems affecting this community either stem from or are aggravated by inequality in the natural resources and economic capacity of individual nations. There are nations that are advanced in their growth and development and nations that are chronically poor (*CCC*, 2437). We are called as a human community to act in solidarity, nation with nation. (*CCC*, 2438). Rich nations have a moral responsibility to assist those that cannot advance economically, helping them to develop and to become politically and economically independent (*CCC*, 2439) so that they enjoy a fair share in "our common home."

Sharing Questions

- How do you see your work, whether paid or voluntary, as a means of sanctification?

- How can you bring the spirit of Christ to your part of society–for example, your workplace or your civic or volunteer organization?

- What, if any, experience have you had of being poor? How does this experience color your attitude toward those who are poor today?

- If you are an employer, what works against your desire to treat your employees with dignity and respect? If you are an employee, how do you give an honest day's work? Share about your work ethic.

Living the Good News

Jesus emphasized the connection between faith and action, between what we believe and what we do. In that spirit, decide on an individual or group action that flows from what you have shared in this session. If you decide to act on your own, share your decision with the group. If you decide on a group action, determine among you whether individual members will take responsibility for various aspects of the action.

You are likely to benefit most from taking an action that arises from your own response to the session. However, you can consider one of the following suggestions or use these ideas to help develop one of your own:

- Make a commitment to improve your work relationship with your employer or employees.

- Jesus always spoke with conviction of those who were poor and the need to love the poor. Who are some of the poor people in your community, and what can you do for them to respond to the challenge of this gospel?

- No action to assist the poor people of the world is too small. What could you do to assist developing countries and help with global economic balance? What steps can you personally take? What steps can we take as a group?

- Think about Zacchaeus' response to Jesus. Zacchaeus gave half of his belongings to the poor. Give something that is very precious to you to a poor person or to an association that helps those who are truly poor.

- Take a walk and thank God for the beauty of creation. Join a group that takes responsibility for safeguarding our natural resources– for example, water, air, soil, forests.

- Create a "miracle of sharing" by offering your gifts to someone in need.

- Become familiar with legislation that will help to feed the hungry. Contact your representatives and urge them to pass such legislation.

- Build a personal relationship with a person from another country who is poor.

In light of this session, this week I commit to:

_____

_____

Lifting Our Hearts

Invite one person to pray Psalm 67.

Follow the Psalm with spontaneous prayers, and conclude with the Lord's Prayer.

Looking Ahead

- Prepare for your next session by prayerfully reading and studying:
    - Session 12: Disciples in Today's World
    - Luke 21:1-4 (the poor widow's contribution)
    - *The Collegeville Bible Commentary: New Testament* by Robert J. Karris, for insight into the passage from the Gospel of Luke.
    - *United States Catholic Catechism for Adults*, doctrinal statements related to the tenth commandment, pages 455-456.

- You may like to consult the *United States Catholic Catechism for Adults*, Chapter 34, "The Tenth Commandment: Embrace Poverty of Spirit."

- You may also like to consult the *Catechism of the Catholic Church*, paragraphs 2534-2557 on the tenth commandment.

- Remember to use Renewing Family Faith and its helpful suggestions on how to extend the fruits of your sharing beyond your group, especially to your families (see page 114).

Disciples in Today's World

The tenth commandment

Suggested Environment

You may have a Bible and a candle on a small table, with the Bible opened to the Scripture text for this session. Next to the Bible, place a "treasure box" and a large cut-out question mark to convey the message "Where is your treasure?"

Consider decorating the table with the color of the liturgical season.

It is helpful to have available the Catechism of the Catholic Church (CCC) *and the* United States Catholic Catechism for Adults (USCCA).

Lifting Our Hearts

Song Suggestion

"Seek Ye First," Karen Lafferty

Prayer

Pray together

Father in heaven,
you call us by name and invite us to friendship
with Jesus, your Son, by the power of the Holy Spirit.
We gather here in Jesus' name.

Help us to overcome our selfishness.
Expand our hearts so that we become true followers
of him who lived for others rather than for himself.

Teach us to believe in your goodness,
to hope for your mercy, and to love our neighbors

by freely sharing with them
the good news and mercy you have given us.
Amen.

Sharing Our Good News

Share how you did with your Living the Good News *from the previous session.*

Reflection 1

A giving frame of mind

Katharine Drexel had it made. She was born in Philadelphia in 1858 to one of the richest families in the United States. Her father, a banker, left her and her two sisters with a trust of fourteen million dollars. Katharine could have done anything with that money, but a strong Catholic upbringing and the example set by her parents had cultivated in her and her two sisters tendencies toward justice and generosity. Katharine decided to create endowments for schools on Indian reservations and, in 1891, she founded the Sisters of the Blessed Sacrament for Indians and Colored People; Katharine was the first sister. She took a vow of personal poverty and insisted that she and her religious sisters live on alms; meanwhile, she dispensed her $400,000 annual income–a fortune in the 1890s–to create and assist missions and schools for native and black Americans. Katharine Drexel died in 1955 at the age of 96 and was canonized by Pope John Paul II in 2000.

Sharing Question

• Few people have the resources that Katharine Drexel had, and few people so completely devote their resources–including their own lives–to the welfare of other people. How do you see her extraordinary story applying to your own life?

"You shall not covet your neighbor's house ... or anything that belongs to your neighbor." (Exodus 20:17)

The literal meaning of the tenth commandment is that we must not steal what belongs to another person. As we discussed in the last session, the commandment goes beyond that literal meaning by forbidding us to wrong our neighbors in any way with respect to their property and by requiring us to treat the material world as something

Spotlight on the *Catechism*

"Some say that helping the poor involves only making sure that all of their physical or material needs are addressed. But is this enough? Should we not also focus on helping people to develop to their utmost potential?

The first step in helping the disadvantaged is to acknowledge the sacred dignity and image of God found in each person. What is also required is a conscience formation from which flow the beliefs, attitudes and actions that will help the poor. Having more is never enough. Being more is paramount.

Christian discipleship means, among other things, working to ensure that all people have access to what makes them fully human and fosters their human dignity: faith, education, health care, housing, employment, and leisure. Members of the Church are called to build up the resources of the Church herself and of civil society in making possible the sharing of God's blessings and social goods with others. This they do by their own generosity in the use of their time, talents, and treasurers with others. Such generosity flows from hearts grateful to God for his generosity in creating and saving us."

United States Catholic Catechism
for Adults, pp. 454-455

that was created for everyone's benefit. The tenth commandment goes even further by addressing a natural tendency in human beings to want things we do not have. We want nourishment when we are hungry, we want warmth when we are cold, we want companionship when we are lonely, we want education when we thirst for skills or knowledge. "These desires are good in themselves; but often they exceed the limits of reason and drive us to covet unjustly what is not ours . . . " (*CCC*, 2535).

So this commandment does not concern only overt behavior, such as stealing; it addresses a *frame of mind* that Jesus emphasized in the Beatitudes. In fact, the very first Beatitude "stated that poverty of spirit would enable us to inherit the Kingdom of God. In other words, the first step on the road to joy begins with a healthy detachment from material goods. Later on in the same sermon, Jesus taught that building up wealth for its own sake is foolishness. We should be more interested in spiritual riches" (*USCCA*, p. 449).

This detachment applies to material goods in general as well as specific goods that belong to someone else. It is a rejection of *greed*–an insatiable desire to accumulate wealth, goods, and property and sometimes the social status and political power that go along with riches (*CCC*, 2536). This desire is encouraged more than ever before by the messages directed at consumers on television, in print, and on the Internet–messages that often are designed to create the impression that a person is not leading a fulfilling life without the latest electronic gadget or motor vehicle. Greed is a distortion of the reasonable desire to obtain what is necessary to care for ourselves and our families (*USCCA*, p. 450). On a larger scale, the "financial scandals that periodically occur in our culture remind us that greed is a constant threat to moral behavior. It leads many to conclude that money is the root of all evils" (*USCCA*, p. 449). But, in fact, "the love of money is the root of all kinds of evil" (*1 Tm* 6:10).

Love of money is the driving force of unscrupulous business practices at all levels, including such things as the low-cost mortgages that contributed to the "great recession" of the late 2000s. Here, again, the commandment addresses our interior life as well as our behavior; the moral issue is not only making an unfair profit on securities, goods, or services, but even *wishing* for conditions that would one an unfair advantage–for instance, a farmer hoping his competitors' crops will fail so that he can raise the price of his own produce (*CCC*, 2537).

Love of money also leads to *envy*, "sadness at the sight of another's goods and the immoderate desire to acquire them for one's self, even unjustly" (*CCC*, 2539). Again, this "sadness" is encouraged by commercial messages that suggest that fictional individuals and families are happy and fulfilled only because of what they own. The *Catechism* points out too that wishing serious harm on a neighbor because of envy can be a mortal sin.

Sharing Question

• Share an occasion when you envied another person's wealth or possessions. How did you deal with that feeling? If you have never felt envy, what has helped you to be content with your own life?

Pondering the Word

"She gave all she had"

Luke 21: 1-4

Sharing Questions

• Take a moment to reflect on what word, phrase, or image from the Scripture passage touches your heart or speaks to your life. Reflect on this in silence, or share it aloud.

• In the gospel passage we just heard, the rich put in their "extra," and the widow put in everything she had. In what areas do you feel called to give more than your "extra"?

Reflection 2

"Strive first for God's kingdom"

When Jesus blessed the "poor in spirit" in the Beatitudes, he didn't necessarily mean poverty that could be measured in terms of cash or acreage or livestock. He didn't mean that people should not own things, nor did he define what constitutes too many possessions or too much wealth. Jesus meant that people should not be absorbed in whatever possessions they have while they neglect worship of God and do not care for their neighbors. Jesus grieved for the rich, not because of their wealth in itself, but because he knew that so many of the rich found their satisfaction only in their abundance, not in God and not in charity (*CCC*, 609).

When Jesus called attention to the widow in the temple, his point was that all people should contribute to the general welfare as that woman did–not from their excess, but from their substance. From those who had more, more was expected. St. Katharine Drexel provided a good example. She inherited an enormous amount of money, but even though she was raised in the upper strata of Philadelphia society, she was brought up with Catholic moral principles. She did not spend the money on herself, but used it to assist people who were being neglected by society and government. That's what Jesus expected of the "poor in spirit," and that's the ideal that the tenth commandment implies.

Jesus made clear his desire that his followers would share and act on his compassion for people who in some way are in need (cf. *Mt* 19:21, *Luke* 14:13, *Lk* 16:19-31). He challenges us with a clear mandate in the Beatitudes and in his vision of the Last Judgment, in which people are condemned not for acts but for neglect. In fact, Jesus' solidarity with those in need is so great that he identifies them with himself: "just as you did it to one of the least of these who are members of my family, you did it to me' (*Mt* 25:40). Mother Joseph and her community acted on this obligation in a dramatic way, but women like them are not the only missionaries in the church. On the contrary, *all* of us Christians are called to be missionaries. All of us are called to *live* what we believe.

In these four seasons of *Why Catholic?* we have reflected on prayer–our conversation with God; on faith–what we believe about God and his Church; on the sacraments–how we celebrate the mysteries of our salvation; and on Christian morality–how our prayer, faith, and celebration shape our lives. As we conclude this faith-sharing experience, we can keep in mind the words we hear at the end of each Mass. "Go," the priest or deacon tells us, no matter which form of the dismissal is used, and the word does not mean, "Go to breakfast." It means go into the world outside this church and put into practice the faith we have just shared, go out and be the helper, be the comforter, be the healer, be the peacemaker.

As we conclude this *Why Catholic?* process, we can think of ourselves as being in the same position as the disciples of Jesus were in one day on a mountain in Galilee (cf. *Mt* 28:16-20). Those disciples had heard Jesus transform the commandments given to their ancestors into a Great Commandment not just to obey the law but to be a blessing, a beatitude, a life-giving presence in the world. Now that Jesus had been raised from the dead, those disciples might have been thinking–as we might be thinking–"What next?" And he told them what he tells us now: Go out and take my message and my blessing to all people, "And behold, I am with you always. . . ." (*Mt* 28:20).

No one excluded from our love of the poor

"In loving the poor, the Church also witnesses to man's dignity. She clearly affirms that man is worth more for what he is than for what he has. She bears witness to the fact that this dignity cannot be destroyed, whatever the situation of poverty, scorn, rejection or powerlessness to which a human being has been reduced. She shows her solidarity with those who do not count in a society by which they are rejected spiritually and sometimes even physically. She is particularly drawn with maternal affection toward those children who, through human wickedness, will never be brought forth from the womb to the light of day, as also for the elderly, alone and abandoned. The special option for the poor . . . manifests the universality of the Church's being and mission. This option excludes no one. . . ."

Congregation for the Doctrine of the Faith, *Instruction on Christian Freedom and Liberation*, no. 68

Sharing Questions

• We have reviewed the Ten Commandments in the light of the Gospel. How does the challenge of the Beatitudes surpass the teaching of the commandments?

- Recall and share a time when concern over material possessions or the demands of your business or job prompted you to re-examine your sense of what was most important in your life. If you have had such an experience, how did you restore balance in your thinking?

- This is the final session of *Why Catholic? Live*. How has your experience in these twelve sessions helped you?

Living the Good News

Jesus emphasized the connection between faith and action, between what we believe and what we do. In that spirit, decide on an individual or group action that flows from what you have shared in this session. If you decide to act on your own, share your decision with the group. If you decide on a group action, determine among you whether individual members will take responsibility for various aspects of the action.

You are likely to benefit most from taking an action that arises from your own response to the session. However, you can consider one of the following suggestions or use these ideas to help develop one of your own:

- Reach out in generosity to someone who has suffered a loss or is deprived of the basic essentials of life. Share something that is meaningful to you with that person or group.

- Celebrate in a special way with your group through prayer or a social event and discuss how you will continue as an ongoing small Christian Community."

- Consider using RENEW International's PRAYERTIME resource for faith sharing on the Sunday gospels. See details on page 116.

- Receive the Sacrament of Penance, and forgive those who have wronged you.

- RENEW International offers a Faith-Sharing Edition DVD of *Scenes from a Parish*, a film by James Rutenbeck, with a guide for building faith-sharing sessions. In Session One, we reflected on one aspect of that film–the experience of Elvys Guzmán, a Dominican immigrant whose life was altered when he discovered the love of Jesus. *Scenes from a Parish* portrays the lives of Elvys and other members of St. Patrick's Church as it copes with change. The film shows how the effects of immigration and poverty challenge the compassion and creativity of the congregation. RENEW's program helps us see how the issues at St. Patrick's are relevant to our hometowns and parishes. See details on page 115.

• To learn about other faith-sharing titles available through RENEW
International, visit www.renewintl.org

In light of this session, this week I commit to:

_____

_____

Lifting Our Hearts

The group stands in a circle.

Song Suggestion

"We Are Called," David Haas

Prayer

Leader	Almighty God, we thank you for the time we have spent together in this community. Through our sharing on prayer, on the sacraments, on the mysteries of our redemption, and on the commandment to love you and each other, we hope to be more closely united to you and to the whole human family.
All	**As we conclude these sessions, we ask you in your Holy Spirit, to help us carry the fruits of our faith, our prayer, and our reflections to anyone outside of these walls who needs our welcoming presence, our comforting words, or our material help.** **We ask you to give us the courage to bear witness to the Gospel especially by speaking out for social justice and working to build it in our communities and throughout the world in any way we can.** **Be with us as we go in peace to love you and serve you.**

The leader places his hands on the head of the person to his right and offers a brief, spontaneous prayer of encouragement to live the gospel by uplifting the lives of others. The imposition of hands and spontaneous prayer are repeated until everyone has participated.

Leader   And now let us pray together in the words
                our Savior gave us.

All recite the Lord's Prayer and conclude with a sign of peace.

Looking Ahead

- Between seasons of *Why Catholic?* you may decide to continue meeting to faith share. Consider using *PRAYERTIME: Faith-Sharing Reflections on the Sunday Gospels.*

- Remember to use RENEWING FAMILY FAITH and its suggestions on how to extend the fruits of your sharing beyond your group, especially to your families (page 113).

- View and discuss *Turning Points: Witness Stories,* a RENEW video series at youtube.com/user/turningpointsstories

- Read our inspirational reflections at blog.renewintl.org

Appendix

Key Themes of Catholic Social Teaching

Reflections of the U.S Catholic Bishops

The Church's social teaching is a rich treasure of wisdom about building a just society and living lives of holiness amidst the challenges of modern society. Modern Catholic social teaching has been articulated through a tradition of papal, conciliar, and episcopal documents. The depth and richness of this tradition can be understood best through a direct reading of these documents. In these brief reflections, we highlight several of the key themes that are at the heart of our Catholic social tradition.

Life and Dignity of the Human Person

The Catholic Church proclaims that human life is sacred and that the dignity of the human person is the foundation of a moral vision for society. This belief is the foundation of all the principles of our social teaching. In our society, human life is under direct attack from abortion and euthanasia. The value of human life is being threatened by cloning, embryonic stem cell research, and the use of the death penalty. Catholic teaching also calls on us to work to avoid war. Nations must protect the right to life by finding increasingly effective ways to prevent conflicts and resolve them by peaceful means. We believe that every person is precious, that people are more important than things, and that the measure of every institution is whether it threatens or enhances the life and dignity of the human person.

Call to Family, Community, and Participation

The person is not only sacred but also social. How we organize our society in economics and politics, in law and policy directly affects human dignity and the capacity of individuals to grow in community. Marriage and the family are the central social institutions that must be supported and strengthened, not undermined. We believe people have a right and a duty to participate in society, seeking together the common good and well-being of all, especially the poor and vulnerable.

Rights and Responsibilities

The Catholic tradition teaches that human dignity can be protected and a healthy community can be achieved only if human rights are protected and responsibilities are met. Therefore, every person has a fundamental right to life and a right to those things required for human decency. Corresponding to these rights are duties and responsibilities— to one another, to our families, and to the larger society.

Option for the Poor and Vulnerable

A basic moral test is how our most vulnerable members are faring. In a society marred by deepening divisions between rich and poor, our tradition recalls the story of the Last Judgment (*Mt* 25:31-46) and instructs us to put the needs of the poor and vulnerable first.

The Dignity of Work and the Rights of Workers

The economy must serve people, not the other way around. Work is more than a way to make a living; it is a form of continuing participation in God's creation. If the dignity of work is to be protected, then the basic rights of workers must be respected— the right to productive work, to decent and fair wages, to the organization and joining of unions, to private property, and to economic initiative.

Solidarity

We are one human family whatever our national, racial, ethnic, economic, and ideological differences. We are our brothers' and sisters' keepers, wherever they may be. Loving our neighbor has global dimensions in a shrinking world. At the core of the virtue of solidarity is the pursuit of justice and peace. Pope Paul VI taught that "if you want peace, work for justice" (Paul VI, *For the Celebration of the Day of Peace* [January 1, 1972]). The Gospel calls us to be peacemakers. Our love for all our sisters and brothers demands that we promote peace in a world surrounded by violence and conflict.

Care for God's Creation

We show our respect for the Creator by our stewardship of creation. Care for the earth is not just an Earth Day slogan, it is a requirement of our faith. We are called to protect people and the planet, living our faith in relationship with all of God's creation. This environmental challenge has fundamental moral and ethical dimensions that cannot be ignored.

This summary should only be a starting point for those interested in Catholic social teaching. A full understanding can only be achieved by reading the papal, conciliar, and episcopal documents that make up this rich tradition. The complete text of *Sharing Catholic Social Teaching: Challenges and Directions* is available online at www.usccb.org/sdwp/projects/socialteaching/socialteaching.shtml

Text is drawn from Sharing Catholic Social Teaching: Challenges and Directions (Washington, DC: USCCB, 1998) and Forming Consciences for Faithful Citizenship: A Call to Political Responsibility from the Catholic Bishops of the United States (Washington DC: USCCB, 2007); available on www.faithfulcitizenship.org

Small Christian Communities

Many people who have been in RENEW faith-sharing groups continue to meet on a regular basis. Through their desire to grow spiritually and the commitments they make to one another, they become continuing SCCs. The remarkable growth of small groups and communities in our time, and the highly positive diocesan evaluations of RENEW small groups in terms of the spiritual growth of parishioners, motivate us to encourage and expand this type of vibrant faith experience.

We envision SCCs as part of the larger parish, indeed of the whole Catholic Church, the people of God, its tradition, teaching, leadership, and guidance. These parish-based communities exist in relationship to the authority of the local pastor and bishop, and they benefit from their role in the larger Catholic Church by living the life of the Spirit.

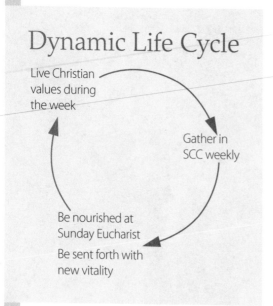

Dynamic Life Cycle

Live Christian values during the week

Gather in SCC weekly

Be nourished at Sunday Eucharist

Be sent forth with new vitality

To realize this vision, the pastor and staff need to give priority to it. With so much else going on, they need to discern and select outstanding leadership for their SCCs, give moral support and encouragement, and entrust the leaders with the implementation of the vision.

While speaking of the value of SCCs, we do not intend to make that value exclusive or to devalue other experiences. No dynamic in and of itself can renew the church. Ultimately, it is the Spirit of God who renews the church. Yet we believe that the recent increase of small communities is one of the more significant events of our age to encourage the renewal of the church and the transformation of the world.

Ultimately, community is a gift. It is not human effort that will build SCCs. It is the Spirit of God working in and through all of us who will set hearts aflame and bring us into communion with one another, with all creation, and with God.

The love of Christ impels us (see 2 *Cor* 5:14).

Why Catholic?
Resources from RENEW International

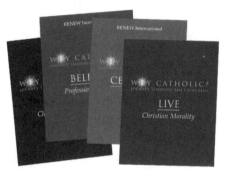

WHY CATHOLIC? Journey through the Catechism is a parish-based process of evangelization and adult faith formation from RENEW International. This process, designed for sharing in small Christian communities, is structured around exploring the important truths of our faith as they are presented in the *Catechism of the Catholic Church* and in the *United States Catholic Catechism for Adults.*

WHY CATHOLIC? helps nourish faith and enhance our sense of Catholic identity. The process and materials encourage us to understand and live the reasons why we are Catholic, and so lead us to a faith that is experienced more authentically, connecting us more deeply and meaningfully to God, and to others.

For each of the four *WHY CATHOLIC?* books, there is a music CD. Each CD is a 12-song compilation of the songs suggested for the moments of prayer during the faith-sharing sessions. The CDs are available singly, or as a set.

Families can extend the fruits of sharing on the same themes presented in the books by using *RENEWing Family Faith:* attractive four-color companion bulletins with activities and reflections for sharing among different age groups.

This process of faith-building through faith-sharing is also available in Spanish: *¿POR QUÉ SER CATÓLICO?*

Additional Resources

There are additional resources designed to foster the fruitful implementation of *WHY CATHOLIC?* and any faith-sharing process:

LONGING FOR THE HOLY: Spirituality for Everyday Life
Based on selected insights of Ronald Rolheiser, OMI

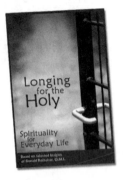

Suitable for small community faith sharing or individual reflection, *Longing for the Holy* covers different dimensions of contemporary spiritual life for those who want to enrich their sense of the presence of God and develop a deeper spirituality.

The Participant's Book contains twelve sessions with prayers, reflections, sharing questions, and stories from saints and contemporary people of faith. This resource is also available in a four-CD set audio edition, which has both narrated text and songs for all twelve sessions.

The songs suggested for the moments of prayer in the faith-sharing sessions are offered on this 13-song CD.

A kit is also available that includes the essential ingredients to bring this engaging spiritual experience to your parish or small Christian community.

Scenes from a Parish
Special Edition DVD and Film Faith Sharing Guides
In English and Spanish

Get a rare glimpse into one parish's real-world experience as it struggles to reconcile ideals of faith with the realities of today's diverse culture.

Reflect on and share faith with this film and *Faith-Sharing Guide* and its themes of welcoming the stranger, offering compassion, and feeding the hungry.

Ideal for parish-wide, small group, and personal viewing and reflection.

PRAYERTIME CYCLE A, B, C: Faith-Sharing Reflections on the Sunday Gospels

This faith-sharing resource responds to the U.S. Bishops' suggestion that "every parish meeting can begin with the reading of the upcoming Sunday's Gospel, followed by a time of reflection and faith sharing."

With each Sunday's Gospel as a focus, PRAYERTIME proposes meaningful reflections, focused faith-sharing questions, related questions for consideration, and prayers as a source of spiritual nourishment and inspiration.

Use PRAYERTIME any time of year, whenever the small community needs. It is also ideal for beginning meetings of the pastoral council, staff, and other parish groups. The themes can also be read personally as a way to prepare for Sunday Mass.

This invaluable resource is also available in Spanish:

OREMOS Ciclo A, B, C: *Reflexiones sobre los Evangelios Dominicales para Compartir la Fe*

GLEANINGS: A Personal Prayer Journal

Many participants in small communities tell us how much they are helped in both their shared discussion and their personal reflection by the technique known as journaling: keeping a notebook for the expression of thoughts and ideas.

Gleanings is a valuable tool for both avid and occasional journal writers. Each page spread is decorated with a spiritual quotation or musing that can inspire prayerful reflection on your relationship with God. The comfortably-sized format makes it an excellent companion for your personal faith journey, helping tap into the richness of God's wisdom within you. It is also a thoughtful gift for friends or family.

For more information or to order these and other fine faith-sharing resources, please visit our secure online bookstore at www.renewintl.org/store or use our toll-free order line: 1-888-433-3221.

PrayerTime Cycle A, B, C:
Faith-Sharing Reflections on the Sunday Gospels

This faith-sharing resource responds to the U.S. Bishops' suggestion that "every parish meeting can begin with the reading of the upcoming Sunday's Gospel, followed by a time of reflection and faith sharing."

With each Sunday's Gospel as a focus, *PrayerTime* proposes meaningful reflections, focused faith-sharing questions, related questions for consideration, and prayers as a source of spiritual nourishment and inspiration.

Use *PrayerTime* any time of year, whenever the small community needs. It is also ideal for beginning meetings of the pastoral council, staff, and other parish groups. The themes can also be read personally as a way to prepare for Sunday Mass.

This invaluable resource is also available in Spanish:

Oremos Ciclo A, B, C: Reflexiones sobre los Evangelios Domincales para Compartir la Fe

Gleanings: A Personal Prayer Journal

Many participants in small communities tell us how much they are helped in both their shared discussion and their personal reflection by the technique known as journaling: keeping a notebook for the expression of thoughts and ideas.

Gleanings is a valuable tool for both avid and occasional journal writers. Each page spread is decorated with a spiritual quotation or musing that can inspire prayerful reflection on your relationship with God. The comfortably-sized format makes it an excellent companion for your personal faith journey, helping tap into the richness of God's wisdom within you. It is also a thoughtful gift for friends or family.

For more information or to order these and other fine faith-sharing resources, please visit our secure online bookstore at www.renewintl.org/store or use our toll-free order line: 1-888-433-3221.